The Writing Workshop

VOL. 2

BY ALAN ZIEGLER

Teachers & Writers Collaborative
5 Union Square West, New York, N.Y. 10003

Funding for this publication has been provided by The New York State Council on the Arts and the National Endowment for the Arts.

Teachers & Writers Collaborative programs and publications are also made possible by funding from American Broadcasting Companies, Inc., American Stock Exchange, Atari Institute for Educational Action Research, Avon Products Foundation, Inc., Chemical Bank, Consolidated Edison Company, The Equitable Life Assurance Society, General Electric Foundation, The Hugh M. Hefner Foundation, Mobil Foundation, Inc., Morgan Guaranty Trust Company, Morgan Stanley, New York Foundation for the Arts, The New York Times Company Foundation, Henry Nias Foundation, Overseas Shipholding Group, Inc., Helena Rubinstein Foundation, The Scherman Foundation, and Variety Club.

Library of Congress Cataloging in Publication Data

(Revised for volume 2)

Ziegler, Alan.
    The writing workshop.

    Bibliography
    1. English language—Rhetoric—Study and teaching. 2. Creative writing—Study and teaching. 3. English language—Composition and exercises—Study and teaching.
I. Title
PE1404.Z5   1981   808'.042'07073   81-16741
ISBN 0-915924-11-0 (v. 1)
ISBN 0-915924-07-2 (v. 2)

For Harry Greenberg and Larry Zirlin
For Nick and Mary Kay Bozanic

ACKNOWLEDGMENTS

A good editor is demanding and sensitive; wise and caring. Ron Padgett is a good editor. I thank him.

I also thank the following for commenting on parts of this manuscript in various stages of development: Sherry T. Barry, Tracy Chamberlain, Christian Hanson, Nancy Reiser, Michael Schwartz, and Cheryl Trobiani (who edited *The Writing Workshop: Volume I*).

Most of my work with children the last few years has been for Teachers & Writers Collaborative at P.S. 75 (Manhattan); I am grateful to Lou Mercado, principal, for his commitment to the Teachers & Writers program, and to the teachers with whom I've worked, notably Carole Karasik. Some of the ideas in this book were also developed in the Lynbrook School System; at P.S. 11 (Brooklyn) and P.S. 173 (Manhattan); as writer-in-residence at the Interlochen Arts Academy in Michigan; and at workshops sponsored by the New York State Poets in the Schools program (Myra Klahr, Director) and Poets & Writers, Inc.

Writing may be lonely work, but teaching writing isn't. Many good people have kept me company, starting with Richard Perry and Barbara Siegel — my T&W teammates at P.S. 11 — and including scores of classroom teachers and thousands of students.

Thanks to the Atari Institute for Action Research for providing Teachers & Writers with word processors that nudged me — not quite kicking and screaming, but twitching a little — into the computer age.

CONTENTS

PREFACE

The Writing Workshop: Volume I emphasizes process in writing and the teaching of creative writing; the focus of *Volume II* is product (in the context of process). Most of the assignments are adaptable for all grade levels, but teachers of lower elementary students will have to pick and choose. Designed for classroom teachers, these assignments can also be used by individual writers.

This is not a clinical, step-by-step "how to" book; I do not lay out a program of writing assignments to be used verbatim and sequentially. Some of the material is discursive, containing thoughts and information I discuss with my students. I want the spirit behind writing to emerge from my classes, and from this book: a spirit of openness, that writing can accommodate the serious and the whimsical, the exotic and the familiar, the cerebral and the emotional. Good writing, whether it's a poem or an essay, is *interesting* (arousing curiosity and concern); I hope that this book is not only useful but also can be read with interest.

The voice I use for the most part addresses "you" as the teacher, but at times it addresses "you" as a student or writer; and, to avoid an overabundance of constructions like "Tell the students to...," I have written parts directly to the students. These sections are italicized. Thus, "Now ask the students to write brilliantly and succinctly" would read *"Write brilliantly and succinctly."* These parts are not intended for use as scripts, but for easier reading.

Above all, make these assignments *yours*. Expand, alter, and combine them to fit you and your class. While they can be presented "off the rack," they'll fit better with your expert tailoring.

I have included examples with many of the assignments; student authors are identified as elementary (E), middle school (M), and high school (HS).

INTRODUCTION

This book deals with what you might say to students in order to inspire them to write. I suggest that these activities be presented in the context of a writing workshop that emphasizes all phases of writing, from conception to completion; provides feedback and support; and encourages individual initiative. A writing curriculum should induce, not constrict, growth. Most of these assignments can be fulfilled with brief or extended pieces of writing — poetry or prose.

Some creative writing teachers shun the word *assignment,* thinking it too authoritarian to be associated with art. But no replacement has caught on, just as no consensus has been reached over such substitutions for *boyfriend* and *girlfriend* as *lover, old man/lady, paramour,* and *the person I live with.*

One alternative for assignment is *topic,* but that lacks a sense of process. Other labels for writing assignments are: *writing ideas, explorations, sparks, tasks,* and *triggers.* (In jest I have suggested calling them *boyfriends and girlfriends.* There are similarities: they can be good company and loving, or remote and unfaithful.) I find myself falling back on *assignments;* if the atmosphere of the workshop is open, if the teacher is encouraging, and if possibilities and alternatives are explored, it doesn't matter what you call them.

•

Blues singer/song writer Bukka White, when asked how he writes songs, replied, "I just reach up and pull them out of the sky — call them sky songs — they just come to me."

If it were only that easy, we could swagger into class like John Wayne entering the Rough & Rumble Saloon and say, "All right, pardners, reach for the sky." But all too often, writers reach for the sky and come up empty-handed (then it's time to sing the blues). Students often need an external spark to ignite writing. Writers use instinct, experience, and talent to take the first step of the creative process: finding potential material. A good assignment is anything that helps students take that first step.

There are those who say creative writing can't be taught through assignments, that the writing teacher's job is only to respond and encourage. Novelist Mark Harris was once asked by his department chairman to give assignments to his college workshop. Harris later wrote in the *New York Times Book Review,* "I couldn't teach writing that way, I had never *assigned topics* before...I expected every writer, however young, however inexperienced, to assign himself/herself his/her own topics, to discover sources by soul searching, by examining their own unexamined lives, etc. One could only be there waiting when the student, inspired by his reading, decided to write something of his own."

Self-assigned writing is a goal to work toward. I present assignments with the hope that they will become increasingly unnecessary. But although a writing workshop without *any* assignments or direction from the teacher may work at the college level it would probably be disastrous on the elementary and secondary levels. Indeed, even highly experienced writers need outside help from time to time. Recently, I got a call from a friend who has published a novel and numerous articles. "Assign me something!" she implored. "Give me something to do to get me going again."

Some critics of assignments claim, "You learn to write by writing." Correct premise, wrong conclusion. If you learn to write by writing, then anything a teacher can do to get students writing is teaching writing. There are some students who will thrive with or without assignments, but we can offer even these special students more than the "space to write"; we can help them learn how to shape that space.

The common denominator of all writing assignments is that they inspire writing. Virtually anything that gets students writing is worthwhile, contributing to their growing facility with language. The value of an assignment often derives more from the experience of writing than from the product.

This book is written in the belief that there is only one writing assignment—"Write"—but that there are endless subdivisions, some of which follow.

PART ONE

ABOUT ASSIGNMENTS

1
Assignment Strategy

This book presents three categories of assignments: Openers, Orientations, and a Catalogue of Assignments. I recommend that you spend time with all of the Orientations (you can vary the order), and choose at random from the other two categories. Planned assignments can be interspersed with Open Sessions, a group creative process leading to a collectively designed writing assignment.

Openers

The Openers are geared for quick success to help the workshop get off the ground in a non-threatening way and are especially useful if some students have a negative attitude toward writing or an insecurity about their ability to write. These Openers can generally be set up and completed in less than 30 minutes, leaving time for reading some pieces out loud or for another quickie. Students can volunteer to read their own pieces, or you can collect the papers and read a sampling (authors should indicate at the top of their papers if they don't want their names mentioned).

The Openers introduce bite-sized portions of themes and approaches that will be useful in subsequent assignments. A few Openers will give the workshop momentum as students gain confidence and begin to feel their writing folders thicken.

Orientations

The next sequence consists of what I call Orientations, which draw on the various "places" that writers get ideas from. Writers constantly tap the following overlapping Orientations: Experience, Observation, Metaphor, Emotion, Communication, Invention, and Language. Devote at least one session to each of these, during which students write a piece based on the

Orientation of the day.

Students get the feel of an Orientation through discussion of the particular idea and several examples of it by professional and student writers. I talk about literary techniques as they arise in these discussions, so that literary and linguistic terms emerge in relation to living pieces of work, not in separate lectures devoid of context.

The Orientation classes provide students with a spectrum of writing experiences; as with the color spectrum, these Orientations can be combined to form unlimited possibilities for future writing. The approaches used in these assignments will constantly be drawn upon in responding to other assignments: a piece about a place will need observation skills, and a poem about loss will include the expression of emotions. Also, anytime a student is stuck for something to write, he or she can think in terms of the Orientations: "Did I observe anything recently I can write about? Are there any experiences I had in the past that could make for an interesting story? Is there something I want to communicate to someone?"

Catalogue

After the Orientations, select from the Catalogue of Assignments. Some assignments can be synchronized with other areas of study, the time of year, or anything else going on in the students' lives. For example, after a class saw a dance recital, I did the Gesture and Movement assignment. Cross-reference assignments when appropriate, reminding students of previous writing experiences that can inform the current assignment.

Although it is hoped that students will find most assignments to be pleasurable, others may be merely tolerable or even somewhat painful. Even the most devout writers embrace some tasks and endure others. But, like food that doesn't taste good but is good for you, less desirable assignments may have beneficial effects in the long run.

On the other hand, just as assignments can call on students to *create* something out of nothing or *re-create* something from the past, it is also important for students to have the opportunity to *recreate:* be playful and have fun with words. Writing should be taken seriously, but that doesn't mean that one has to write seriously all the time. Assignments can have no "point" other than to be enjoyable, which is an important part of the total language experience.

The Catalogue of Assignments introduces students to topics that have been constant objects of writers' attention. Once students have gone through a couple of dozen of them, they will have a feel for the wide range of writing possibilities and various ways of approaching them.

Many of these assignments are designed to be repeatable. Because a student has responded to the Appreciation assignment doesn't mean that there will never be anything else to appreciate. When students ask, "What should I write?" one way of answering is to suggest that they go back through the assignments they have already done and pick one to approach from a different angle.

4

2
Assignment Making

Narrowing The Field

W.H. Auden said, "It takes little talent to see clearly what lies under one's nose, a good deal of it to know in which direction to point that organ." Assignment-making generally consists of narrowing the field of literary vision so that students can spot a starting point. It may seem that facing a blank page with a blank mind is the writer's worst problem, but the problem is really that there is *too much* to write about. Everything we have ever experienced, seen, felt, or imagined is "research" we have done for writing; there is perhaps no other artistic activity that the average person is more prepared for. But students often don't *recognize* what there *is* to write about, or don't know how to bring a vague notion into focus.

An assignment should narrow the field while opening up a range of possibilities within that field. We should help students aim and focus, but not tell them what to see. The degree to which any given assignment narrows the field depends on the purpose of the assignment and the needs of the students. For example, an Observation assignment with a wide range might be: "Go for a walk for 15 minutes and write about anything interesting you see." The field could be narrowed further: "Write about *two people* you see on your walk," or even narrower: "Write about two people from the knees down—their shoes, cuffs, the way they walk."

Many of the assignments in this book contain specific suggestions for narrowing, which you can use to help students become acquainted with the narrowing process; when possible, students should participate in the narrowing. For an assignment on Growing Up in New York City my students isolated the following directions in which to point their noses: crime, fun, graffiti, housing projects, welfare, landmarks, subways, crazy people, and discos. This menu enabled students to aim their pencils at specific targets, and because the choices were self-generated the responses were more authentic than if they had come from a prefabricated ditto sheet.

The more experienced a writer, the more natural the narrowing process becomes, although some accomplished writers consciously use narrowing techniques. Novelist William Burroughs has used a device that literally narrows his field of vision. He would go for a walk, focusing on a specific color, trying to block out all other colors. Once, he saw a truck painted the particular color, and on the truck was a word that triggered a memory that evolved into a section of a novel. With an unrestricted field of vision, Burroughs might not have noticed the truck at all. His restriction led to an opening, and Burroughs knew how to recognize and exploit the emergent subject matter.

Students can use a pre-narrowed assignment as a device for finding the "real" subject. When students restrict themselves to the assignment, and do not explore, words fill the page — providing valuable writing experience and a honing of skills — but the students do not experience the crucial "discovery" aspect of writing. Highly restrictive assignments, which have come to be known as "gimmicks" — or, more cynically, as "stimulus/response" exercises — do have a place in the writing curriculum. They are good for limbering up, developing confidence, and dealing with writer's block (which one of my students referred to as "lockwrist"). But they are not the main event.

I try to find that famous but elusive happy medium by heading students in general directions without mapping out their courses; assignments should be invitations, not itineraries.

When the writing teacher veers away from highly structured assignments he or she risks disorder and frustration. I've made the mistake of relying on student self-reliance before the class was ready for it and, in so doing, I was not giving the students what I had to offer. Occasionally fall back on games and gimmicks. Lighten up the atmosphere; then students can return to the darkness refreshed.

Distractions

You need not be subverted by distractions in the classroom; something strong enough to distract a class might engender a writing assignment. A few students in a high school class were having a hard time concentrating, buzzing back and forth instead of writing, and I asked them what was going on. They replied that they were in the school play, which was to open that evening. I suggested that they write about that experience, and we discussed several approaches to narrowing the field, including: relationships among cast members, crew, and the director; such physical sensations as makeup, lights, and costumes; and the range of emotions an actor experiences from audition to performance. I suggested that the following week they could also draw from opening night, closing night, the cast party, and postpartum feelings. Student athletes and musicians can use similar approaches to writing about a forthcoming or recent event that is distracting them.

One rainy November afternoon, I was about to start a session with third graders when I saw, for the first time that year, snow. How could I compete with the first snowflakes of the year, as they delicately salvaged a gloomy day? A student spotted the snow and ran to the window, followed infectiously by half a dozen others. I'd never seen the class so genuinely excited.

"Sit down, this is time for poetry!" the teacher yelled, meaning well. "Come on, you've all seen snow before." But we hadn't seen snow for eight months, and there had been very little snow the winter before. This was the only "first snow" we would have, and it would probably last a mere few minutes before turning back into rain. I felt ambivalent about the snow: it was beautiful and brought back some warm winter memories, while contrapuntally it foreshadowed moats of dirty, ankle-high slush off curbs and the return of the wind-chill factor to the weather reports.

My heart was with the kids scrambling for position at the window, and, being writers, we could have our cake and eat it: I let us have our few minutes with the snow, followed by a discussion that mobilized the diffuse excitement, converting this distraction into an assignment. We discussed how reunions, "first times," and snow-induced memories could be turned into writing.

Food is a common source of distraction, particularly during 11:00 A.M. classes. A couple of fifth graders were discussing their lunches, and one responded "Yech" to what the other would be eating. I told them that cooks, like writers, juxtapose simple ingredients to get complex results, and asked them to conceive of "yech food combinations." They cooked up some rather strange — often disgusting — sandwiches and platters, including ingredients not found in the most open-minded chef's pantry:

> Raisin bran with smushed potatoes; birdseed and apple turnover; nine pig eyes; a cake with pickle and sardines...

Mistakes can be considered a kind of distraction, but you can learn from most mistakes, and others you can downright exploit. In James Joyce's *Ulysses,* Stephen Daedalus says of Shakespeare: "A man of genius makes no mistakes. His errors are volitional and are the portals of discovery."

"Benevolent mistakes" include mishearing and misreading. While a class was writing, I misread an envelope on the teacher's desk as being addressed to the "Director of Dreams." I quickly realized it was "Director of Drama" and mentioned my mistake to the class, adding, "Now, 'Director of

Dreams'—that's an interesting job." One student, who had been having trouble getting an idea, embarked on a story about the holder of that position. (The Director's office in the story was "Room 17"; on my way out, I noticed a film projector marked "Room 17." You take what you can get, then you make something out of it.)

Hints

Henry James described the impulse for *The Spoils of Poynton* as "a single seed, a seed as minute and windblown" as a "casual hint...dropped unwitting" by his neighbor. Of course, the "seed had to be transplanted to richer soil," but the first step was to take the hint.

Playwright Peter Shaffer tells of passing a stable with a friend, who was reminded of a crime he had heard about; the friend's "complete mention of it could barely have lasted a minute—but it was enough to arouse in me an intense fascination." Shaffer did not seek elaboration on the incident, for he "knew very strongly that I wanted to interpret it in some entirely personal way. I had to create a mental world in which the deed could be made comprehensible." Shaffer's ignorance of the real events enabled him to explore and discover, and the seed flowered into *Equus*. A brief anecdote gestated in the writer's imagination and was transmuted into a full-scale work.

Sometimes a "hint" is not used directly in the work. Vladimir Nabokov described the "initial shiver of inspiration" for *Lolita* as being prompted by a newspaper article about an ape in a zoo who, "after months of coaxing by a scientist, produced the first drawing ever charcoaled by an animal: this sketch showed the bars of the poor creature's cage." Although there is no textual connection between this anecdote and *Lolita,* it got Nabokov started.

The world abounds with hints for writing ideas; likewise, the classroom supplies them for writing assignments. One way to conceive assignments is to listen to the students the same way Henry James, Peter Schaffer, and Vladimir Nabokov listened to the world. You can pick up hints for writing assignments even though the students don't know they are hinting. When you turn a hint into an assignment, let the students know what you're doing, to help them internalize the process by which hints are exploited.

A high school student had the same expression on her face as her paper—blank. She looked at me as if I were stepping on her toes and she muttered, "Pain, agony, I don't know what to write."

I replied, "Write about someone who is in pain and feels helpless. Does the way you feel now remind you of a way you have felt before?" Now she looked at me as if I had riveted her toes to the floor, but at least she could think of her pain as a departure point rather than a destination.

Virtually everyone in the fifth grade class was writing, but Daama's paper was still wearing its birthday suit. As I passed by he smiled sheepishly, and I said, "A bad day at the word factory?" Daama's instant response was "The word factory is closed for repairs," which stopped me in my tracks:

"There's your beginning." Being a slow writer, Daama wrote only a few lines by the end of the period, but he continued in subsequent sessions. A picked-up hint and perseverance combined to produce his most developed piece of writing.

As you read through student papers, look for a phrase or image that can spark another piece of writing. Chrissy Keller, a fifth grader, used the phrase "the long gone past forever" in an otherwise forgettable poem. I suggested that she write a poem using that line as the title. The new poem ended "they will always knock/ at my brain forever," a lovely image which she might not have otherwise written. A high school student wrote an undistinguished piece about a friend's younger sister. The last line leaped out at me: "A smart one, yes, a smart one, but she learned a few things before her time." That was where he ended, but to me the last line was a beginning. A fourth grader wrote the phrase "arguments in my head"; I assigned the group to use that as a springboard.

Also be on the lookout for students' special experiences or unusual aspects of their lives, which may seem commonplace to them but be exotic to others. I suggested that Titus Dixon, a fifth grader whose father is a preacher, write a piece in the form of a sermon:

> This is a question I ask to myself and I'm going to answer it! How did poetry come into the world?
> I believe poetry came into the world when God made it. Poetry was almost anything and is almost anything. I believe poetry is like the wind blowing and withering the flowers of the earth. It also is the salt of the earth that makes it lively. The animals and all creeping insects are all poetry for the earth. Poetry is laughter, happiness, meekness (like a lamb going to slaughter). It is also wild and fierce like the dinosaurs and cavemen long ago.
> Poetry keeps you, poetry is sometimes happiness, madness, sadness, and gladness. It is like the morning dew which wets the ground and purifies it. It is like the sweet smelling rose, and like the odor of clean air.
> I believe poetry is clean, it is cleaner than the soap we use, it is purifying and is a preservative to the body we have on. I believe it is also a shield of defense and a rod of protection, and a happy and joyful feeling.
> —Titus Dixon (E)

Some of the assignments in this book are designed to produce hints for future writing. For example, responses to the Parade and List assignments might contain images or ideas that deserve further attention.

3
Assignment Presenting

Imagine Blake or Shakespeare visiting your classroom. There would come a time during the period when a student would ask, "But, Mr. Blake, what are we supposed to *write* today?" or "Mr. Shakespeare, what's the *assignment*?" Such masters, under the pressure of several workshops a day, might formulate their approaches into packaged assignments: Blake asking his students to "write a poem with a vision in every line," and Shakespeare assigning dialogues, "imagining that your mother is the queen and your stepfather the king."

Some good writing would come from such assignments no matter who presents them, but I suspect that Blake and Shakespeare's presentations would capture the *spirit* as well as the "P's and Q's" of the assignments. To some extent, there is a "cult of personality" at play here; an assignment that elicits wonders by its enthusiastic originator might induce yawns if someone takes it out of a book and presents it mechanically. In this book I provide only the anatomy of assignments; you must make them come to life by making them *yours* as you present them.

The Set-up

I have a fairly high tolerance for varied activities taking place during workshops, but I ask the class to strive toward the platonic ideal of unanimous enraptured attention while I am setting up an assignment. I suggest to students working on writings other than the day's assignment that they listen to the set-up anyway for future reference; if they choose to write during the set-up, they must do so inaudibly if not invisibly.

The set-up consists of two parts, which are sometimes interwoven: the teacher's presentation, and questions/discussion. I tell students: "During my presentation, we both have jobs to do. My job is to describe an idea for writing and to conjure images related to that idea. While I am talking, your job is to be an active listener: to visualize the images being presented, personalize details, and fill in any blanks. Then, your job is to remain active during the ensuing discussion, whether you are directly contributing or not. Together, our job is not only to crystallize a writing idea, but to create an atmosphere in which you *want* to write."

You can preface the discussion/questions segment by asking a student to paraphrase briefly what you have just said. This helps you know if you're getting through, and it gives students a second shot at understanding the assignment. You can kick off the discussion by asking, "What else *could* I have said?" encouraging students to amplify your ideas.

Find the optimum moment to turn from discussion to writing. A truncated set-up might result in a chorus of "Huh's?"; going too long can deplete the time and energy for writing. When the discussion is on the verge of peaking, with hands going up like exclamation points, you can say, "Put it on the page instead of saying it."

The set-up corresponds to all or part of the prewriting phase of the writing process; many students begin writing immediately afterward, while others need more time to mull. Emphasize to students that the set-ups often contain more possibilities than they can handle, especially in one sitting. I often toss around numerous ideas and angles, hoping that one or more will connect with every student.

Samples and Influence

My set-ups often include professional and student sample writings, to help students perceive possibilities. Rather than avoid professional literary material with words or references that students won't understand, I prepare the class by giving footnotes in advance ("headnotes"?) for important words and phrases. For the purpose of the assignment students need not understand every word.

As you use these assignments, keep copies of your students' writings to incorporate into your subsequent presentations. Students should understand that a sample illustrates just one possible response and is not comprehensive or definitive.

After writing, a student might say, "I did it wrong, mine isn't like the ones you read," to which I respond, "Terrific, I've already read those; now I'll have something different to read." Other students model their writing too closely on a sample. A resemblance is all right—a distant cousin, not a clone. I do not criticize a student who borrows an element of a sample and adds a new dimension. Classroom distractions and time limitations put a lot of pressure on students; to prohibit students from borrowing elements from the samples is too demanding.

It's exciting for students to think that their work might be appreciated by and perhaps influence other writers. I've seen work by fourth

11

graders influence high school students years later. One eighth grader was disappointed that he had only a two-line poem in the school literary magazine, until I told him that it had influenced others.

Here's an example of a positive use of influence:

Jealousy

The feeling is coming
I know it by now
My face gets hot
my eyes start to close
my fists get clenched
then the tears start to come
I hate her
I cry
not meaning a thing
I wish I were dead
They don't love me at all
they love her more
I try to tell myself that's wrong
They love me, too
but I find myself
crying too hard to believe myself.
Then I calm down
and try to smile.
It worked
I'm happy again
all of a sudden they love me
again.
                              —Karen Halfon (E)

Jealous

When I am jealous,
my body shakes
and my throat feels
like there is a rope pulling me.
Then the water comes out of my eyes
like it is raining
over my face.
I stomp up to my room and smile.
I wash my face off,
everything is almost better,
but my throat still hurts.
That little bit of jealousy, never
seeps
out
of
my
brain.
                              —Jennifer Agro (E)

12

Jennifer would not have written her poem without exposure to Karen's. I had felt dissatisfied with the unconvincing ending of Karen's poem, and Jennifer took the idea one step further by dealing with the fact that a "little bit of jealousy" always remains.

Success

A gardener who plants dozens of seeds doesn't expect each one to sprout. Nor should the writing teacher expect each assignment to be exploited to the hilt by every student. I don't consider it a failed session if only twenty percent of the students come up with something sparkling. If an assignment is a complete bust, I try to figure out what happened. Sometimes it's due to class chemistry for that particular day, and the same assignment soars when tried again later.

Teachers & Writers Magazine used to have a section called "Failures" because of the belief that "descriptions of teaching 'failures' are as enlightening as glowing accounts of success — if not more so. The success stories often slough over subtleties of process and style which don't command attention until they trip the teacher up." You might want to devote a session with students or colleagues to assignments that didn't work well. Try to determine if the problem arose from the conceptualization or the presentation. Such frank discussions with students will foster an atmosphere of openness and trust, reinforcing the notion that no one has total command over writing or the teaching of writing.

4
The Open Session

Open Sessions utilize group process to arrive at assignments collectively. Several of the assignments in this book were originally developed through Open Sessions, like the way comedians build routines out of ad-libs and improvisations.

French poet Max Jacob pointed out that John D. Rockefeller, when asked how he had become so wealthy, replied, "By looking to see how a fortune could be made out of every object that I touched." Writers are on the lookout for riches of a different sort. The question "What should I write?" probably ranks right up there with "What do you want to eat tonight?" on the list of most-asked questions. In the Open Session, students collectively figure out how a wealth of writing can be culled from anything around or inside them. Finding an impetus is the first step in the creative process; during the Open Session, students and teacher take that step together, as students participate in the process by which writing assignments are perceived, seized, and shaped.

My most exciting teaching, as with my writing, often comes when I am not sure what I'm going to do next — when I surprise myself and allow the students to surprise me. Sometimes I go in with a beginning point (an image, idea, or poem) and develop it with the class into an assignment; other times I ask the students to supply the departure point: "Okay, I'll let someone else start this one. Anyone have a flicker? You can start with a general subject area, an observation or experience, or a single word." Push for details, images, and associations. You can play "word association" (going around the room, with each student saying the first word that comes to mind), which you can expand to "image association" (students give clusters of words). An Open Session can lead to an assignment for individual use or for a class collaboration.

14

Your job during the Open Session is to keep the discussion going; to write key ideas on the blackboard (using circles and arrows to make connections — the board may wind up looking like a complex literary equation); and, when the foundation is solid and momentum strong, to summarize what has been said and to articulate the writing possibilities. You can act as facilitator or full-scale participant, rejecting or combining suggestions and adding your own. Try an Open Session early in the term to illustrate how associative thinking can coalesce into writing ideas. As the class becomes attuned to this group process, you will have to do less.

I've started Open Sessions by saying, "Tell me something I don't know." "What's the first thing that comes to your mind?" "What's new?" Or "Did anything interesting happen to anyone lately?" If someone starts to tell an anecdote, you can stop him or her in the middle and ask another student to pick it up from there. If a single story line develops, you might want to assign chapters to individuals or small groups, or let everyone share the same premise. Or, you can work through the whole piece verbally, with students taking notes and fleshing it out later.

Recently, I've started Open Sessions with such concepts as "being hurt" and "bullies." In the "being hurt" session, we talked first about the kinds of ways we get hurt, both physically and mentally. The discussion took flight when we focused on how people respond to someone who is hurt, and that's what most of the students chose to write about.

I started the "bully" class with an anecdote from my childhood about a neighborhood bully, and followed it with several minutes of discussion about physical bullying. I then pushed (bullied) the conversation toward other possible sources of intimidation, such as popularity, intelligence, wit, and positions of authority (official or unofficial). One student mentioned that people bully their pets, which I countered by pointing out how a dog can bully its owner out of the house early on a cold Sunday morning. When I stopped the discussion, most of the students had ideas for vignettes or stories. I suggested that anyone who was stuck could list situations in which one person bullies another, or could free associate with the words on the board, including *boss, pick-on, bother, manipulate, hit,* and *insult.*

If a few students tend to dominate Open Sessions, you might have to orchestrate wider participation. But I try not to badger reluctant students; some writers do not function well in this kind of setting.

From Planned Lesson to Open Session

The most carefully devised and presented writing assignment can end up like a party host's unsuccessful call for everyone to dance; you stand there with your hand out, but no one moves. Conversely, sometimes a lesson plan unravels, but the loose strands transfigure into something equally or more worthwhile; or a quirk of discussion turns a smoothly proceeding planned lesson into an Open Session. Just as you can exploit felicitous discombobulations in your writing, you can alter or drop a prepared assignment to pursue a new possibility.

I was presenting an assignment about Places when I mentioned that the names of stores and restaurants can be clever or revealing. "For example," I said, "there are restaurants in Los Angeles named Hollytolly Pasta House and Mexicatessen." One of the sixth graders mentioned the City Dump, a cornucopian store in Manhattan. Several students laughed at the name, finding it strange to title a store after a garbage depository.

I told them about a rural dump I had been to, which is divided into three sections: trash, recyclables, and items that other people might find useful (broken furniture, old toys, etc.). People sift through this last pile for anything salvageable; in effect, they shop at the dump, which, like its New York namesake, is full of surprises.

New Yorkers—not having such a dump—often abandon useful items, especially furniture, on the sidewalks. I told the students about an antique rug I had found, which, after some repairs and a cleaning, fit nicely in my apartment. The discussion rambled on about things that we throw away that others find useful; within a family, such items are known as hand-me-downs. It was suggested that ideas, too, can be handed down, such as the notion of the Tooth Fairy or Santa Claus. One student said, "We also let go of feelings—we stop feeling the same way about a friend," and I added that we "discard" cravings for foods, toys, and hobbies. We don't always have control over such changes, and there are times we know we *should* discard something—an idea, a friend, a toy—but we just don't want to. Sometimes we let go of things and want them back (did the person regret throwing out the rug I found?).

The animated discussion could have continued all period, but I remembered my calling and we articulated several writing possibilities dealing with throwing things away and letting things go. This was one of the results.

Things I Got Rid of

My old notebook—
It collected dust.
Now I need the notes.

Half of my sandwich—
I was full.
Now I'm hungry.

Some old dolls—
They got boring.
I want to play with them.

My old block set—
My mother always tripped over them.
I love building houses.

Some of my poetry —
I wanted to be organized.
Now I want to read it.

When I get a Bazooka
wrapper I'll always
think twice before I
throw it away.

                — Sasha Edwards (E)

From Open Session to Planned Lesson

Sometimes an Open Session will play right into the hands of a stock assignment. I started one Open Session with the familiar gambit, "What's new? What's happened since I saw you last week?" One of the fourth graders reported that her snake had run away; another told me that her mother's godmother had died; and a third said that their teacher, who had been absent for a couple of weeks, would be gone for the rest of the year. All of these anecdotes dealt with loss, and I eased into the Loss assignment, tailoring the set-up to the experiences of these particular students.

Talk

If a class is suffering from an epidemic of writer's block or a case of energy diffusion, sometimes it is better to let up rather than push harder. Instead of playing the taskmaster ("You've got to settle down and write, write, write!") or the cheerleader ("Hey, gang, where's that old literary spirit?") it might be better just to *talk* with the students. You can talk about writing, or you can explore what's on their minds, including local and national news issues, social and family situations, or just unfocused chitchat.

This might turn into an Open Session, but even if the discussion doesn't lead to an immediate assignment, it might inform future writings. Sometimes it is best not to leave the realm of discussion; the class and you might need a breather from writing, and this is a way to get to know each other a little better.

Literary Triggers

Occasionally I start an Open Session with an evocative poem or prose excerpt, approaching the discussion with a spirit of exploration, instead of acting as a tour guide to preconceived conclusions. I frame the conversation with such questions as "What has the writer achieved, and how has language achieved it?" and "What possibilities are suggested for your own writing?"

This poem by Michael Benedikt suggests two assignments:

Go Away

Go away, go away, and as soon as you come back
Be something better.

For example a shell — one that has lain for days on the edge of a beach,
        overturned and sparkling, light captured on an edge,
An oak-leaf-like cluster of sunlight that filters through elm branches,
An earring bobbing, like a float at high tide, against the neck of
        somebody very sweet,
A weatherbeaten motheaten coverlet,
Or the arrows on the arm of a diving suit or a space suit indicating
        where to thrust through the arms.
Think: in reference to the mainstream of human desires and wishes
What would you know now, if you briefly waved goodbye to the world?

One possibility is for students to assume the identity of one of the objects Benedikt mentions in the poem (a "weatherbeaten, motheaten coverlet") or any other object. Another is to use the last line as a stepping-stone: what would you do if you "briefly waved goodbye to the world"? What would you "know now" as a result of waving goodbye?

Chinese Ink Stick

I was a Chinese Ink Stick. I had always been handled and moved. Cold staring eyes looked at me every summer morning when the cool winds came and the elephants passed by. I sat on a felt-covered shelf surrounded by pencils, silks and other fine writing implements. I one day fell onto a rug. Oh, how soft, finally I am alone. It feels so good I can smile to myself and be in a vast small civilization. I was enjoying a little half-covered part of a rug. I was finally able to get thoughts about everything. My ink was circulating calmly. I liked ths new life compared to those big, small funny hands feeling me all the time. Suddenly my master (owner of the store) stepped on me with his big black heel. My ink poured out. I still felt wonderful to have been able to catch a few moments by myself. I drew a picture of a cloud with no winds ever touching it nor the sun shining on it. I was able to because I felt in a way the cloud felt.

— Jeffrey Kosakow (M)

Sometimes I use a piece of writing by a student to start an Open Session. The author, if he or she is in the class, may be surprised and delighted at the complexity of the discussion; writers often don't realize how smart they are until smart critics let them know.

The following poem by high school student Barbara Green can serve as a springboard for a lively discussion (the interesting linebreaks are discussed in *The Writing Workshop: Volume I,* p. 57):

The Key

A thin stream (winter's
snow) runs down the
gutter. Naked trees

towered over the st-
reet casting shad-
ows. New songbirds
clean their nests.
As I walk the side-
walk, I am enchanted
locked out of my ho-
use writing this do-
wn on the back of
an old paycheck
stub.

The persona, locked out of her house at the confluence of winter and spring, finds herself observing things she might not have otherwise noticed. The title is ironic: her lack of a key becomes the metaphorical key to turning adversity into enchantment. Being "locked out" can be discussed on literal and meta-phorical levels:

What would you do if you were locked out? What might you discover in your neighborhood that you hadn't noticed before? Would the initial enchantment turn to annoyance, then to fright? Whom would you turn to? Would you knock on the door of that peculiar old lady on the corner with the pet snakes, whose house no one dares enter? Would you swallow pride and call on the friend with whom you've had a falling out and sworn never to talk to again?

Other than not having a key, why might you be locked out? Has someone inside locked you out? What discussion would you have with that person, your bodies pressed against the locked door. As you get angrier and angrier, the person inside might say, "Be quiet, the neighbors will hear you!" and you shout, "I don't care if the whole neighborhood knows!" (This could be explored via dramatic improvisation, and a short play could result.)

What are metaphorical equivalents to being locked out? How do people lock each other out with their bodies and behavior? Have you ever been locked out emotionally or spiritually by a friend or family member? Military academies have used the "silent treatment" as a severe punishment; how would it feel to be ostracized at school? Would you befriend an outcast even if it meant possibly being locked out by the popular kids? How would you cope?

Some people lock themselves in by closing themselves off from others. A story could be written about someone who literally locks himself or herself in a room (one by one, friends and family knock on the door and try to convince the person to "come out of there"), or about someone who does it figuratively by refusing to reveal himself or herself to others.

Numerous ideas for poems and stories can be gleaned from Barbara's brief poem about being locked out. The important thing in an Open Session is for such a poem to act like a stone thrown into a lake, radiating ideas during classroom discussion; don't lock yourself into one set departure point for an assignment.

PART TWO

OPENERS

5
The Party

When first meeting with a group, I used to have the students tell a few things about themselves. Little of substance tended to be revealed, and I would forget most of the information. But when I asked a group of students to introduce themselves with all lies, the responses were more memorable. Out of this I developed the following scenario, which I ask students to visualize:

You are at a party. There are lots of impressive people there, none of whom you have ever met before. The guests boast of their accomplishments —athletes, royalty, artists all. The host turns to you and says, "Well, we haven't seen you before. Who are you?" The room falls silent, the guests turn toward you, waiting for your response.

Write a paragraph or poem introducing yourself to the gathering, using any combination of lies and the truth. You can fantasize about who you would like to be, or you can say wild things to tantalize or provoke the guests. Reality is not in force—you can exaggerate your exploits, even over a period of centuries; you don't even have to be human. Or, you can "be yourself"—but present yourself in a compelling way.

This icebreaker assignment can be done in a few minutes or longer. Then, ask volunteers to "introduce" themselves as if they were at the party; you can play host, interjecting comments like "Pleased to meet you...and who might *you* be?" This sample includes an elaboration of the set-up:

I got up from my seat at the banquet table to get myself a martini. I dropped in a maraschino cherry. As I pulled out my chair to sit down it made a shrill scraping sound. Talking stopped, heads turned, toasts died out and 4,200 pairs of eyes stared unblinkingly at me. There were several low murmurs of things like, "Who's that?" "I've never seen it here before," and "I wonder what great thing it's ever done." I knew it was up to me to speak and so I began:

"Ladies and gentlemen of Famed Minds, Rich People and Other Famous People, it is an honor to be here. Obviously you have never seen me before and so you may well wonder at me. What great feat have I accomplished? I'll tell you.

"I have no name, but call me Ima Dreme. With my form unlike what you've ever seen before in reality, I am only seen in the nightmares of all you closed-minded matter-of-fact fools; this is what I am to you. While I'm the most beautiful dreams of those who keep their minds and hearts open to possibilities and impossibilities. This is what I am to them.

"I was sent to take you all on a journey through the land in which I live. You will travel through the region of my home encountering many things. I live in the depths of the unknown and rarely come out into this harsh world of known logical idiots. I do now, though. You'll do well to wonder why."

— Allison Gunn (E)

These Party characters can be used throughout the term as characters for short stories or personas for poems or diaries. You can mimeograph information on the characters and turn them loose on the class. A newspaper can be written about them, including news stories, interviews, gossip columns, editorials, and reviews, possibly with the Party characters interacting.

6
Visual Comparisons

The making of comparisons is something language can do more directly than other art forms. For this assignment, limited to visual comparisons, students flex their imaginations in preparation for the more fully realized comparisons to follow. This assignment also sharpens observation skills and acquaints students with the powers of juxtaposition.

Make a visual comparison between two objects without explaining the comparison (Don't say "The sun looks like a ball because it is round"); do not be afraid to make outrageous comparisons. Write as many as you can in ten minutes. Don't worry about "duds."

Fluorescent lights look like icecube trays.
A blackboard is like the ocean at night with fish leaving foam trails.
Composition paper is like a swimming pool with racing stripes.
— Various Students (E)

7
The Most Amazing
Things. . . .

Sources for creative writing constantly lurk around the outskirts of language and the imagination; people write outrageous, impossible occurrences. But the "real world" is amazing, too. This exercise deals both with invented and real "amazing things."

First, ask the students to write "The Most Amazing Thing I've *Never* Seen" (write this phrase on the board). They can make up anything, as fantastic and unlikely as their imaginations will allow; the wilder, the better.

Then, ask how this assignment can be re-oriented by removing one letter: by erasing the "N" we now have "The Most Amazing Thing I've *Ever* Seen." Now the task is to write something incredible but real. Rule out anything seen on television or in the movies. Students don't have to go for splashy spectacles; there are many simple miracles we take for granted, and the writer's job is to isolate these moments and present them sharply.

> The most amazing thing I've never seen
> was an angel
> with long brown hair
> fluttering in back of her
> sliding down a rainbow
> with clouds surrounding her.
> — Jeffrey (E)

> The most amazing thing I've never seen
> was a dentist wearing purple
> eating cotton candy

and putting marshmallows in his ears
giving candy to his patients
and mixing taffy with the toothpaste.
                    — Jenny Klein (E)

The most amazing thing I've ever seen
was when I fell down the stairs
because I was in the
middle of the air.
My face
was facing
the floor.
                    — Jenny Lewis (E)

The most amazing thing I've ever seen
was a pan fry in a stove
and the pan had a chicken in it.
The chicken was sizzling.
                    — Anonymous (E)

This assignment suggests numerous variations. For example, "The Most Heroic Act I've (N)Ever Seen" would elicit invented stories about metahuman feats, and narratives of real people exhibiting physical and/or emotional courage. Other variations include "The Most Horrible" or "The Most Beautiful Thing I've (N)Ever Seen."

8
The Power of Words

Words have power. "Sticks and stones can break my bones, but words can never harm me" is sheer propaganda. Most kids suffer less from a bruised shin than a battered ego, and a well-placed compliment can be a lasting gift.

Think of a time when someone used words that affected the way you felt about yourself or something that was going on, making you feel happy, sad, hungry, excited, nervous, relieved, etc. What was the context in which the words were spoken? Make the reader understand why the words were powerful to you.

Ask for a few verbal responses, followed by writing.

The most effective thing that anyone has said to me in the last two years or so happened last year. It didn't change the way I live, but it did change the way I thought about things.

It happened pretty late in the school year. My teacher, Ms. Dworman, was talking to me. I was worried about letting someone go because I thought I'd lose them. Her exact words were, "The best way to hold on to someone is to let them go." Whether she made that up or heard or read it somewhere, I'll never know. But I know that I'm graduating this year and I won't feel as bad as I would have a year or two ago.

—Anna Belenki (E)

9
Feelings: Do Something About Them

If you are in a restaurant, very hungry, and tell the waiter, "I am starved, famished," he will sort of know what you are feeling, but he won't know what you want to *do* about it. On the other hand, if you say, "I want to eat a double cheeseburger, large fries, apple pie, and a milkshake," then you'll get some action. Your feeling of hunger is differentiated from that of the person who orders tossed salad, broiled chicken, sauteed vegetables, and frozen yogurt.

This assignment links emotion with action.

Take one or more feeling-words (such as hate, love, or anger) and write what someone might do to express each feeling. You can include realistic actions ("Anger: punch my brother") and impossible ones ("Excited: jump from rooftop to rooftop, singing"). They don't have to be things you would really want to do. Make sure you stay in the realm of physical action. Try to visualize what you are writing.

You might complete the following sentence: "When I am angry (or loving, sad, etc.) I would like to---" (This is easier but formulaic. Perhaps the best way is for the student to title the piece with the emotion and then not mention it in the body of the piece.)

As you go around the room while the students are writing, encourage specificity. If a student writes, "I would break something," ask, "What?" If the student replies with something possible ("break a window"), you might suggest adding an exaggeration ("break a bus"), and vice versa. Also ask, "Then what?" The following example started out with three lines. A series of "then whats" helped it grow into a nicely developed poem.

29

Mad

My mouth burns up.
I jump so hard
I fall through the floor.
When I hit the bottom
Of the earth,
It echoes through the universe.
When I tell my mother,
She understands the life I'm in,
Tells me I can stay up late.
I hope I get mad
A lot more often.

—David Patterson (E)

When I feel stupid
I want to bang my head on the wall
to get my brains moving,
to take them out of my head
and paint them a different color.

—Anonymous (E)

10
Go Somewhere

Close your eyes and "go somewhere"; write about where you went.

This assignment gets students to make something out of nothing and describe that something. It also demonstrates the open-ended nature of writing. Emphasize that there are no incorrect responses.

After the group has written, ask students either to read their responses or briefly summarize where they "went." Then point out the different kinds of places, dividing them among real places the author has actually been to ("my grandmother's house"), real places the author has never been to ("the North Pole"), and imaginary places ("a brightly lit tunnel which led to a room full of animals reading books").

One teacher complained to me that when she tried this assignment "half the class went to Disneyworld, and the other half to Disneyland." If this happens to you, ban temporarily such predictable places and try it again.

11
Word Combining

*Write five or six words you have strong feelings about; you can like
or dislike the sound or meaning of the words. Or they could be words that
for some reason happen to be sitting around in your head, like a word from
a popular song that you find yourself humming. You don't even have to
know the meaning of all the words.*

*Now write a short, unrhymed poem (4-6 lines) using all the words,
not necessarily in the order you wrote them down, and not necessarily one
pre-selected word per line.*

*You needn't take this any more seriously than a little puzzle, though
your results might be interesting and contain thoughts and images you can
use for future writing.*

(kitten, respiration, sensuality, sympathy, Anne, Rasputin)

Anne is a sex kitten. She is well
known for sensuality. I, Rasputin,
feel great sympathy towards her, for
some day her respiration will stop.
—Carolyn Kintish (HS)

(love, peace, moose, tolerate, be)

You just called me a moose
but I will tolerate you
You don't know how to be yourself
I can't blame you
so I wish you love
but not too much peace
—Cindy Gerbitz (HS)

(accelerating, haughty, cat, wisdom, destruction)
The haughty cat got in her plane
and flew at an accelerating speed,
and, using her wisdom, narrowly
averted destruction.
                    — Eric Thompson (HS)

There are several variations on this. One is for students to write phrases they hate to hear said to them (It's time for bed; castor oil; Hurry!) and love to hear (Surprise!; I love you; You can stay up as long as you like). They can write a poem for each list, or one poem combining the two.

•

According to a Yale University study, the twelve most persuasive words in the English language are: "save, money, you, new, health, results, easy, safety, love, discovery, proven, and guarantee." Write a poem using most or all of these words; or, make a list of the "most beautiful" (or disgusting, conceited, pretentious, threatening, scary, etc.) words and use these words in a poem.

Try this exercise with images →
hateful, tender, exciting, etc,
   | | |
 knife   hand   ferriswheel

12
Dreams

Dreaming is our peephole into the unconscious. We all dream several times a night, and dreams are more easily remembered when you think about them in the morning or write them down. I find that paying such attention to my dreams tends to make subsequent dreams more interesting. Perhaps the unconscious does better when it has an audience.

Many authors have used their dreams in their writing, altering the original dream material to varying degrees. Transcribing dreams is a good way to get acquainted with inventive writing and can be particularly beneficial for students whose work tends to be constricted or predictable. In dreams, all laws are subject to repeal, including the laws of nature and human behavior. People who died ten years ago are allowed to live again, at whatever age and in whatever shape the unconscious chooses.

Students' dreams might be laced with symbolic overtones, but it is not the teacher's job to interpret or analyze them, even when a poem like the following comes along. This was the author's first piece of substantial writing; he was happy and proud to have written it, either unaware of the psychological implications or fully aware of them and glad to get the poem out of his unconscious. His mother had recently remarried.

Once I was having a dream
which had all kinds of silly
things in it. It was interrupted
by the changing of keys. I got up
and pulled out my pea-shooter
which I always hide underneath
my mattress. Next I heard him open
my door and I thought to myself

and said I think I will shoot his
eyes out. When he was close enough
I shot his eyes out. I woke up
thinking that I'd see a monster
missing two eyes and lying on
the floor. I saw my father
lying on the floor with his
eyeballs lying on the floor across
the room. What a terrible sight
to see.

—Anonymous (E)

Writing about dreams can open the door to the unconscious, a room some students are reluctant to enter. This poem, dealing with that dilemma, might make for a good classroom discussion.

The Journey to The Dream

Once there was a girl named Gina who never dreamed. She felt different and rejected. One day when she was sleeping she got up and walked around her room. Then her head came off her body and she walked into her head. When she got into her head she saw a whole bunch of doors, marked: memory, private stuff, and dreams. She was so happy that she opened the dream door and went inside. Inside were things like dead people, scary music, and monsters. She ran out and connected her head back to her body. After that she was glad she was different and didn't dream. Along with the good, there is always some bad.

—Denise Mazzella (E)

•

Write a dream you remember.
Complete either line: "Tonight I would like to dream———" or "Tonight I would be afraid to dream————"

13
Poetry Is Like

An image is a group of words in which the sum is greater than the parts. Any use of figurative language can be considered an image, which generally uses visual and physical language to achieve an effect.

Complete the simile "poetry is like" with an image that conveys any aspect of the possibilities of poetry or your feelings about poetry. Write as many as you can in ten minutes. Since the possibilities for poetry are limitless, so are the responses to this assignment. Don't hesitate to contradict yourself from one image to the next, since one's attitude toward poetry can change from one moment to the next.

Read the responses out loud; usually, several will elicit laughter, especially from younger students. This exercise is quick, easy, and fun. It can set the stage for future activities by letting students know that creative writing is a wide-open field. Also, it is good practice at image-making, without the pressure of finding contexts for the images.

As the students are writing, I scamper around the classroom, reminding them to be specific. For example, the response "poetry is doing something you can't really do" is not an image; it is abstract, with no appeal to the senses. I asked the author to be specific about something he couldn't do, and he wrote "poetry is like tunneling through a rock with bare hands."

When students are stuck, you can use this formula to bail them out: ask them to tell you something they hate and something they love. Then suggest they combine the two somehow. One student responded by saying she loved spaghetti and hated spinach. Then she wrote: "Poetry is like eating all the spaghetti in the world and dumping the spinach into the Atlantic Ocean."

When results are being read aloud, pause to discuss images that say something important about poetry, thus introducing notions that might be helpful later. "Poetry is like mixing a color with another one" makes the point that writers combine words to create new entities.

Students should allow some of the images to form themselves, without consciously trying to say something about poetry. If an image is beautiful or disturbing or in any other way compelling, that in itself makes a point about poetry.

These responses make direct comments about poetry or the creative process:

Poetry is like:

a world in a head
combing your hair when you're in a rush
newborn pains in the neck
closets opening and closing
when your fish jumps out of the fishbowl to see what it's like out there
a stick of dynamite that's going to keep blowing up no matter what
touching a cactus without being stung
the moon because it floats all over the world
the times of your sloppy life
painting without paint
something falling out of the sky, it's very fragile, you want to catch it
      before it breaks
when a person runs into another person shopping
when you feel like your brains have drained down to your feet

The following are good images that would not have been born without this assignment; they can be used in future writings:

a hamster running under a bed
the sadness when you see a kitten and you're not able to touch it because
      you're allergic
a clown sinking in the sand
smelling the taste of strawberry ice cream
looking at a puppy in the window of a closed pet shop
a pizza on the blackboard
going into the woods and listening to the giggling of the streams
a leaf dripping off a deer

One of my favorite responses to this assignment is one which, although it doesn't meet my definition of an image, says a lot about the power of poetry: "Poetry is finding out that you're not really dumb."

14
Titles

Students should visualize the following (which you can embellish):

It is twenty years from now. You are a celebrated author, known particularly for your prolificness and versatility. You have recently published your memoirs, and a national magazine is doing a cover story about you. The reporter is interviewing you in your private study. (At this point, ask the students to suggest what the study would look like and what it would contain; what would be on the desk, in the drawers, on the walls, etc.?)

One bookshelf is devoted to your own works. You have written books in virtually every genre—sometimes just to make some fast money while pursuing more artistic endeavors—including novels, poetry, self-help, how-to, travelogues, cookbooks, philosophy, religion, and sports. The reporter asks you to name your favorites.

Make up titles of your books in several genres; write as many as you can think of (you can do more than one title in a genre), including at least one novel, one book of poems, and your memoirs. Remember, titles help sell books, so they should be enticing and/or informative. Most titles are from one to five words, but some effective titles are much longer. Stay away from such mundane titles as a memoir called My Life *or a book of poems called* Reflections on Life. *The novels category can be broken down into subdivisions, such as mystery, romance, science fiction, and adventure.*

Before you teach this assignment, peruse your own bookshelves and make a list of interesting titles to read to the class. My shelves feature such enticements as: *The Punished Land, One Hundred Years of Solitude, Dismantling the Silence, Friends You Drank Some Darkness, Secrets & Surprises, Winner Take Nothing, The Wishing Bone Cycle, Tell Me A Riddle, Lugging Vegetables to Nantucket,* and *The Baron in the Trees.* (I tend to give simple, but, I hope, resonating titles to my own books, such as *So Much To Do* and *Planning Escape*). Since I don't own any self-help books, I went to a bookstore and discovered the following titles: *The Silva Mind Control Method, The Act of Selfishness, Peace of Mind Through Possibility Thinking, The Art of Hanging Loose in an Uptight World,* and *Creative Aggression.*

    Students should copy their invented titles onto the inside covers of their writing folders, for future use. One student eventually wrote something for all his titles, checking them off as he went along. One workshop never went beyond this assignment, which we did on our first day. Each student embarked on a semester-long writing project stemming from one of the titles, resulting in mini-novels.

> Novels: *Undeveloped Film; Private School Cool* (Young Adult); *Love on the First Flight* (Romance); *Monstrous Infants; Invasion of the Foam Snatchers* (Horror); *The Man Who Became a Clown; Center Child; The Flowers Died When You Did; The Mess and His Cousin, Too.*

> Poetry: *Rampage on the Brainstorm; What's at the End of the Rainbow; Get Out of My Backpocket.* (The last one was serendipitous: as a student was reading her titles out loud, a classmate put his hand into her backpocket; she uttered this phrase, and I said, "Great title!")

> Memoirs: *They Made Me Do It; My Skinny Body; Reflections in a Mud Puddle; What, It's Done?; How I Abused Myself With Love, Money, and Relatives.*

> How-To: *How to Help Yourself Go Crazy; One Hundred Ways to Use Eyelashes.*

> Cookbooks: *The King of Oatmeal; Hair Cooked Just Right; Vegetables and Their Mystery.*

> Self-Help: *What Can Be Learned From Prehistoric Man.*

PART THREE

ORIENTATIONS

15
Experience

To write a history of the Panama Canal, you'd have to go to the library, but to "research" a poem or story you can go directly to your memory (although the brain isn't conveniently organized by the Dewey Decimal System). We tend to forget that we remember so much from the normal (and abnormal) course of living, even if it takes some excavating to get at those memories. Archeologists go on digs to discover the buried secrets of ancient civilizations; think of writing from memory as a dig into your past, in which you'll find artifacts and snippets of experience that can be reassembled.

The Muses are often misconceived as giving free rides to writers; Dante had the proper spirit when he implored the Muses, "Assist me!" The Muses' method of assistance is to prompt memory. (Their mother was Mnemosyne, which in Greek means "memory.")

The extent to which writers rely on their own experiences varies, but you would miss out on a vast resource if you didn't tap this rich mine in the mind. Elizabeth Hardwick's novel *Sleepless Nights* contains this image of the use of memory: "If only one knew what to remember or pretend to remember. Make a decision and what you want from the lost things will present itself. You can take it down like a can from a shelf. Perhaps. One can would be marked Rand Avenue in Kentucky.... Inside the can are blackening porches of winter, the gas grates, the swarm."

Search through the shelves containing your "memory containers." Open the container marked "First Day of School," or the one labeled "The Day My Baby Brother Came Home From the Hospital," or "The First Time I Lied," or any other one that interests you. There are details in your memory container, like Elizabeth Hardwick's "gas grates" and "blackening porches of winter." Pour the contents onto the paper; they may tumble out haphazardly, or they may fall neatly into place, but either way get as much as possible out of the memory container. If you can't remember certain details, you can "pretend to remember."

When you have finished your first draft, turn the container upside down and give it a good shake, to make sure there isn't an image stuck at the bottom. There might be a note cross-referencing this container with another one: the container marked "Summer Camp" might contain a reference to a friend who has a memory container all her own. If one memory reminds you of another one, you don't have to stick with the first one. Follow the leads wherever they take you.

Instead of containers, students can visualize rooms, each with a door indicating which memory is in that room. Urge students to be more specific about their memories than the author of this Experience poem, which *refers* to strong memories but never tells us what they are:

The childhood we came from
The naive girls we were.
The days of reality, where
things are real, transformed
into matters we never thought possible.
Memories shared filled with laughter and pain.
We're waiting for the future's unforgettable memories.

The image of containers or rooms filled with memories is an artificial writing stimulant, but it is tangible and gets results. Many students do not need the "container" visualization, while others get lost in a sea of memories without it.

For younger students, you might draw some containers on the board and label them with memory categories suggested by the students, perhaps starting them off with the ones I mentioned in the set-up.

Thinking back on my younger years is an almost hopeful task. . . . One of the things that comes in clearest to me is one day when I was very young. A day that later became a milestone in my life.

I was feeling bored so I started to nag my mother to read me a book. When she refused I said sulkily that I would read it myself. So not being able to really read, I started looking at the pictures and pretending I knew what it said.

I had this little game of looking at the book and trying to guess what the words were, partly by looking at the pictures and partly by trying to sound out the words. I did this quite often.

I suddenly had an idea. I would really try to read the book this time. Looking at the hopeless mass of words, I started to sound them out. Finally I read the first page. I mean I really read it, not half made it up. After about an hour I finished the book.

My first reaction was that I didn't need my mother to know what books said. Then I looked at the book and realized I had really read it. I had read my first book.

When I was about 10 I gave the book, which was named *Hop and Pop,* to a 3-year-old friend of mine. I read him the book and told him how much it meant to me. He didn't realize its sentimental value but he really enjoyed the story.

—Sam Nisson (E)

When I was five I had to get my hair cut. We went to the barbershop. A tall man stood in the doorway. The way he looked at me made me shiver. He had a large hairy face. A little boy was getting his hair cut. The room was quiet. The man yelled, "Next." I swallowed. I got out of my seat and walked to the stool. He chopped the scissors and started to cut. I watched my hair fall little by little. He started to shave the back of my head. I got goosebumps. He smiled at me in the mirror. He was my worst enemy. He was done. He gave me a lollypop. When I got home my brothers laughed at me. I ran and hid in my room.

—Craig Carson (E)

•

Write about an important relationship you had when you were younger; it could be with a relative, neighbor, or friend. It might be with someone who taught or helped you discover something about yourself, like Sonny Hugg in "The Sleeper" by Edward Field:

The Sleeper

When I was the sissy of the block who nobody wanted on their team
Sonny Hugg persisted in believing that my small size was an asset
Not the liability and curse I felt it was
And he saw a use for my swift feet with which I ran away from fights.

He kept putting me into complicated football plays
Which would have been spectacular if they worked:
For instance, me getting clear in front and him shooting the ball over—
Or the sensation of the block, the Sleeper Play
In which I would lie down on the sidelines near the goal
As though resting and out of action, until the scrimmage began
And I would step onto the field, receive the long throw
And to the astonishment of all the tough guys in the world
Step over the goal line for a touchdown.

That was the theory anyway. In practice
I had the fatal flaw of not being able to catch
And usually had my fingers bent back and the breath knocked out of me
So the plays always failed, but Sonny kept on trying
Until he grew up out of my world into the glamorous
Varsity crowd, the popular kids of Lynbrook High.

But I will always have this to thank him for:
That when I look back on childhood
(That four psychiatrists haven't been able to help me bear the thought of)
There is not much to be glad for

Besides his foolish and delicious faith
That, with all my oddities, there was a place in the world for me
If only he could find the special role.

Poem

On my first day of school
I didn't want my father
to leave me,
but he had to go.
I remember when I sat down
a girl rolled me her pencil
and I rolled it to her.
I couldn't speak to her
and she couldn't speak to me either.
We both didn't know English.
The girl is Italian
and I am Salvadorean.
The girl's name is Silvona.
Then I learned the colors and numbers
and a lot of words
and then the girl could talk to me
and I could talk to her.
                         —Claudia Rodas (E)

16
Observation

Each day we look at thousands of things, but how many of them do we really observe and remember? Could you describe the building across the street from your front door? The eye color of three colleagues? The back of your hand?

Many jobs depend on the ability to observe. A detective will notice clues that you or I might look right through; what may be elementary to Sherlock Holmes is postgraduate work for the rest of us. A doctor distinguishes between a healthy tongue and a sick one; an interviewer, observing that the politician wrings his hands during a response, pursues that line of questioning; a baserunner studies the pitcher for an indication that he is going to attempt a pick-off; and the cook knows the precise moment to turn the omlette. Discuss with the class these and other jobs that rely on the powers of observation.

Joseph Conrad said, "My task is by the power of the written word to make you hear, to make you feel—it is, before all, to make you see," and William Blake wrote, "A fool sees not the same tree a wise man sees." How can I quote Conrad and Blake without adding the subtle pithiness of Yogi Berra: "You can observe a lot just by watching."

•

Students writing from observation often make judgments about what they have observed, without including the stimuli that led to the judgments. For example, the sentence "She walked into the room; she was sad, then she opened the envelope and got happy," tells us that she was sad then happy. What did the writer *see* to know this? What is the writer holding back? It would be stronger (though overdoing it) to write, "She walked into the room as if there were weights on her feet; her mouth was limp. She picked up the letter with tremulous hands, and the words hoisted her lips into a smile. She kicked the weights off her feet and jumped, clicking her heels."

Writers should think of themselves as witnesses at a trial, with the readers acting as judge and jury. Poet Charles Reznikoff put it this way: "Say a person is suing for injuries, and the defense is that he was negligent in crossing the street. The witness isn't allowed to go on the stand and say, 'Yes, he was very careless' or 'He was very careful.' He's got to say just what he did in order that the jury and judge may determine whether he was careful or careless." Writers have more resources than witnesses; we can spice our testimony with figurative language. When a student uses too many unsubstantiated, judgmental expressions like "He is scared" or "She is sleepy," I say, "I object!"

This also goes for describing objects. If someone is on trial for stealing a chair, a witness doesn't help the prosecution by claiming to have seen a chair in the defendant's apartment. However, if the witness testifies that he saw a "beige, leather armchair with a cigarette burn on the left armrest," then the defendant would be either in trouble or cleared.

The impact of a written observation derives from the intrinsic value of what was observed and from the writing itself. Read the class the following excerpt from Annie Dillard's *Holy the Firm*, first asking, "Who thinks a writer could make you get emotionally caught up in the death of a moth?" Most students don't think so, but a slow reading of this passage has often produced audible reactions:

One night a moth flew into the candle, was caught, burnt dry, and held. I must have been staring at the candle, or maybe I looked up when a shadow crossed my page; at any rate, I saw it all. A golden female moth, a biggish one with two-inch wingspan, flapped into the fire, dropped her abdomen into the wet wax, stuck, flamed, frazzled and fried in a second. Her moving wings ignited like tissue paper, enlarging the circle of light in the clearing and creating out of the darkness the sudden blue sleeves of my sweater, the green leaves of jewelweed by my side, the ragged red trunk of a pine. At once the light contracted again and the moth's wings vanished in a fine, foul smoke. At the same time her six legs clawed, curled, blackened, and ceased, disappearing utterly. And her head jerked in spasms, making a spattering of noise; her antennae crisped and burned away and her heaving mouth parts crackled like pistol fire. When it was all over, her head was, so far as I could determine, gone, gone the long way of her wings and legs. Had she been new, or old? Had she mated and laid her eggs, had she done her work? All that was left was the glowing horn shell of her abdomen and thorax — a fraying, partially collapsed gold tube jammed upright in the candle's round pool.

And then this moth-essence, this spectacular skeleton, began to act as a wick. She kept burning. The wax rose in the moth's body from her soak-

48

ing abdomen to her thorax to the jagged hole where her head should be, and widened into flame, a saffron-yellow flame that robed her to the ground like any immolating monk. That candle had two wicks, two flames of identical height, side by side. The moth's head was fire. She burned for two hours, until I blew her out.

The visual artist's ability to capture a scene is called "hand/eye coordination." Utilize "language/eye coordination" to depict any scene. (You might want to write about something of little "significance"—as Annie Dillard did—and make it important.) If there is something emotional going on in the scene, try to make the reader see it, as in this sample, which captures the feeling after a children's party, when all that is left is the mess:

Images

The room is empty now, except for one child.
Paper party hats and candy wrappers
lie haphazardly on the floor.
Streamers hang on the ceiling, making a delicate
bridge from wall to wall.
On the table
spilled soda and melting ice cream
form a dirty river, weaving its way
between soggy potato chips.
Near the child are
ripped wrapping paper and broken bows.
Tears flow down the child's pink cheek.
Dressed in a white suit, he sits clumsily
swallowed by a giant chair
holding in his hands
a dead doll.
                    —Cindy Gelper (HS)

Observation

Images

I look back for the last time.
The fingers of her right hand
Lift the window sill.
Long, pale fingers curl
Like a half-globe.
Her index leads the others up,
With the arc of her arm.
I see the underside of the hand,
Her tender, trembling palm.
                    —Lenroe Hammers (HS)

Look out a window for ten minutes and write what you see.

17
Metaphors & Similes

Entries

When I think no thing is *like* any other thing
I become speechless, cold, my body turns silver
and water runs off me. There I am
ten feet from myself, possessor of nothing,
uncomprehending of even the simplest particle of dust.
But when I say, You are *like*
a swamp animal during an eclipse,
I am happy, full of wisdom, loved by children
and old men alike. I am sorry if this confuses you.
During an eclipse the swamp animal
acts as though day were night,
drinking when he should be sleeping, etc.
That is why men stay up all night
writing to you.
                                        —James Tate

Aristotle wrote that "the greatest thing by far is to be a master of metaphor," and "A good metaphor implies an intuitive perception of the similarity of the dissimilar." In "Entries" the persona squirms with the validity of such similarities. The irony is that the persona must use comparisons to convey the frustration he feels when he doesn't believe in them:

When I think no thing is "like" any other thing
I become speechless, cold, [as if] my body turns silver
and water runs off me. There I am [like I am]
ten feet from myself, [like a] possessor of nothing....

50

Metaphors and similes are so deeply woven into our writing and speaking that we often don't notice them. (The phrase "deeply woven" is a metaphor). When we are scheming something and say, "The wheels are turning," we implicitly compare the brain to a machine. (A computer age version would be to say, "I'm online.") Even an empty comparison communicates an intensity, as this assertion I overheard: "That's ugly as *anything*!" There's a rock group called "Mental As Anything."

An insult such as "You're *crazy*!" is usually a metaphor, not a clinical judgment: "You're acting *like* a crazy person." Our language is laced with clever metaphors for crazy behavior, such as "She's not playing with a full deck," or "He's got a hole in his marble bag" (a spinoff of "He's lost his marbles").

Metaphors and similes work best when they make the reader see, feel, or understand something. They are diversions from the subject at hand that illuminate the subject. In Robertson Davies's novel *Fifth Business,* a returning soldier says, "The war had not matured me; I was like a piece of meat that is burned on one side and raw on the other, and it was on the raw side I needed to work." The subject is a soldier's imbalance of experience, but a diversion into the "meat" simile illuminates that imbalance.

Comparisons are often more memorable than prosaic constructions. "Float like a butterfly, sting like a bee"—Muhammad Ali's credo, originated by his trainer, Bundini—would not be repeated so often if Bundini had phrased it: "Be beautiful and move gracefully, but all of a sudden lash out and really hurt the guy." Bundini's phrase not only sounds good, but is also economical and visual, as is a fireman's description of a blaze going "up like a kite," which simultaneously conveys speed and height. I once wrote in a letter: "Although I have closed the door between us, I have not locked it." After I wrote those words, I realized there was no need to say more.

What is the point of the following poem by David Ignatow? Certainly it is not about a sponge and a lake:

Sediment

You are such a well-rounded sponge
from head to foot
that I have made myself a lake for you
not to see you shrivel up
and I have surrounded you with trees
and a distant view of a mountain,
calm sky above.
No rain comes while you and I float together,
your reflection in me, and then slowly
you settle down, filled.
I think you are going to drown
and I will go dry, utterly absorbed in you,
my mud and rock showing. I worry about us,
you swollen and out of shape
and I tasting of sediment.

51

The metaphor of a sponge and a lake makes the point that one-sided giving in a relationship is dangerous for both people. Ask a student to describe such a relationship without using comparisons; not only is it difficult to do, but it comes out sounding flat.

•

Writers often try to stun, uplift, or move the reader (the writer is a linguistic bully). I've sometimes said to a student after he or she has written a pedestrian poem or story: "I know what you're trying to say, and I care about it because I know you, but you should write in such a way that someone who doesn't know you will get involved." Metaphor can be a powerful device for accomplishing this.

When I was in college I wrote an article for the school paper dealing with sexist attitudes. My ideas were not unique, but I used metaphorical vignettes that, I hoped, would reverberate beyond specific situations. The reaction was startling: a deluge of letters to the editor, discussions in the dining halls and classrooms, and an extremely defensive/offensive reaction by the All-College Council, which censured the editor. Sam Ullman, an English professor, explained the volatility of the reaction by writing sarcastically that "inept abuse can be tolerated, but metaphor menaces and should be shunned." Translation: "metaphor magnifies and should be shined."

I once concluded a review of a play with this arrow: "Watching this production was like eating a whole meal of melba toast—you come away full but not satisfied." (Writers must decide whether to tack an explaining phrase onto a comparison, as I did in this case; ending with "toast" might have greater impact, but the explanation ensures understanding. I tend to feed more to the reader in journalism than I do in poetry. Comparisons, like jokes, can be ruined by too much explanation: a politician recently called someone a "Pinocchio," then went on to say, "He's lying so much his nose is going to grow long, like Pinocchio's did in the fairy tale.") I later heard that the cast and author of the "melba toast" play used some metaphorical phrases in reaction to my review—cursing may be the most prevalent form of metaphor in daily discourse.

I've also been on the receiving end of wounding metaphors. A reviewer compared my first book of poems to a salad without a meal (I suppose it was poetic justice for me to be menaced by a food metaphor). I was deflated by the review but got pumped up by a letter from someone who demonstrated the pliability of language by bending the metaphor: "If your book is a salad, it's a Caesar's Salad." The snarling metaphor now smiled.

A high school student used a "torture" metaphor to communicate his frustration with my asking students to write on demand. His metaphor was more effective than a whining complaint, and it echoes in my mind occasionally when I need to let up on a class:

Sitting, listening and then writing.
"Stroke, Stroke," he yelled,
the whip cracked against my back
"Stroke, Stroke," hit with the whip again.
The water torture started
each drop coming down, screaming
screaming, hitting like a hammer.
"Don't worry, you'll get an idea,
just keep thinking, keep trying,
everybody can write poetry"

Stroke, Stroke Stroke

•

Research into the use of metaphor has found that making metaphors not only helps people organize and communicate ideas, but also aids in the process of discovery. "Scientists use creative analogies and comparisons to extend theories and even to make new ones," writes physicist Roger S. Jones in *Physics As Metaphor*. Alexander Graham Bell compared the human ear to a machine, helping him to conceive of the telephone, and Darwin used a tree metaphor in conceptualizing his theory of evolution. The use of metaphor in science helps confirm the notion that creative writing involves exploration as well as expression.

Characters in stories can make discoveries through metaphorical situations. In a short story, I used the metaphor of a badly tangled knot in a shoelace to represent a badly tangled relationship. After hurriedly trying to untangle the knot with no success, the frustrated protagonist takes a pair of scissors and literally cuts himself off from his problem. The protagonist realizes that quick excisions rather than difficult solutions may free you, but such cuts can take you from one situation to another without teaching you how to cope with problems.

I was discussing writing problems with a class when a student used a metaphor to express his difficulty with writing stories: "I paint myself into a corner." I followed his metaphor in attempting to find a solution: "You would *literally* paint yourself into a corner by unintentially cutting off options — you risk leaving no path out when you paint without an overview. In writing, you can do the same thing by making a move that will trap you in a corner (such as killing off a character who will be needed later). One solution is to backtrack and make a change that will open a path out (have the character decide not to cross the street just before the truck comes barreling down).

Metaphors have been widely used to represent political and sociological situations — shaping the way people perceive the world — including "the domino theory," "the iron curtain," and "paper tiger." At the other end of the spectrum, many comparisons, especially descriptive similes, are no more than window dressing, "full of sound and fury, signifying nothing." Ezra Pound cautioned against the use of comparisons as "ornaments," although I feel that's a matter of taste — some people *like* ornamentation. But too many ornamental comparisons can be gratuitous and distracting.

André Breton, a theoretician of surrealism, favored metaphors in which the two things being compared are as dissimilar as possible in every regard except the aspect being compared, because "the greater the disparity, the more powerful the light, just as in electricity the greater the difference in potential of the two live wires, the greater the voltage." Readers can usually discern the aspect of similarity; for example, when you compare your love to a rose, the reader infers the reference to the rose's beauty and delicacy, not the rose's figure.

Breton was not fond of similes, saying that "Surrealism has suppressed the word 'like' — He who fails to see a horse galloping on a tomato is a fool." Similarly, Hamlet said, "Seems, madam! Nay, it is; I know not 'seems.'"

Whether you like your comparisons with or without "like," wild or tame, similar or dissimilar, as ornamentation or illumination, it is almost impossible to communicate without them. Language without metaphor is like...well, you get what I'm driving at.

Write a short narrative or description, using as many metaphors and similes as possible.

Moving Day

My house, old and weary. It looks like an old man standing straight as a lamp post. Inside I pass my mother's blouse. I see the designs dancing in the forest of wool. I get a funny feeling that they would just jump out and leave the blouse blank. In the living room, the boxes are surrounding me like clumps of trees. My room, empty like a hollow stump. It is so empty it looks like a hungry boy with an empty stomach. Meanwhile, my father is cutting tape in the bedroom. It is so loud it sounds like an elephant screaming its head off. The kitchen, fish sizzling like a snake hissing. The hallway silent as cotton, so quiet the quietness pops your ears. My paper, getting longer and longer, my head getting weaker and weaker.

— Anna Villapando (E)

Write about one situation or relationship in terms of another, as in Ignatow's poem "Sediment" (an extended metaphor). The situation that triggers the metaphor need not be described.

a wave
it swells and grows
rising for the sandy white beach
then it hits

54

smashing the sand
and carrying parts of it back
with her, not leaving it the same.

I'm sorry I didn't mean to do it.
—Elaine Chatson (HS)

For My Grandmother

Awakening one morning with
a full day ahead. Raising your
petals and ready to go. You're
after full bloom, but you act
like just a little bud. We play
water catch. Throwing the water
back and forth through
our fresh roots. Our stems
are green and fresh because
we're taking care of
each other and we keep healthy
when we're happy.
—Lisi Labinger (E)

Since humans are different in so many ways from other animals, a comparison that pinpoints a similarity with an animal can be effective. In Robertson Davies' Fifth Business, *the protagonist tried to explain his fascination with saints to his colleagues, who "looked uncomprehendingly, like cows at a passing train." Write a poem or paragraph that includes a comparison between a person and an animal.*

She walked into the room and sat down, tired from her work today. She looked like a puppy just waking up.
—Nell Waters (E)

The teacher chose me to read my composition in front of the class. The student stared at me like a cat watching a goldfish in a bowl.
—Luke Ratray (E)

As the suspect was questioned, the detective suddenly turned on him saying, "What do you know about Gordon Fence?" The suspect looked quite taken aback and said, "I never heard of him." But the detective looked him right in the eye and could tell that he was acting like a possum playing dead.

The detective tried a different approach and said, "Where were you on the night of December 25?" The suspect answered, "Celebrating Christmas with my dear little grandmother." The detective was now getting as frustrated as a bull who kept missing the bullfighter.
—Allison Gunn (E)

Language Environment

The next assignment — which overlaps with the Emotions section — is to create a metaphorical "language environment." In addition to imagery, there can be narrative development and a sense of place, as in this poem by Gregory Orr:

When We Are Lost

Darkness surrounds the dead tree. Gathering around it
we set a torch to the trunk.
High in the branches sits an old man
made of wax. He wears a garland of wounds;
each one glows like a white leaf with its own light.
Flames rise toward him, and as they touch his feet
he explodes, scattering insects made of black glass.
A moth lands on the toe of my boot.
Picking it up, I discover a map on its wings.

This metaphor for being lost contains movement and a resolution. After a series of images of displacement and pessimism, the final image is one of hope ("Picking it up, I discover a map on its wings"), reminiscent of the saying "It's always darkest just before dawn." Note that the poem never uses the word "lost," but contains images that *correspond* to that predicament. T.S. Eliot coined the phrase "objective correlative," which he defined as "a set of objects, a situation, a chain of events which shall be the formula of that *particular* emotion; such that when the external facts, which must terminate in sensory experience, are given, the emotion is immediately evoked." Which translates to: without writing directly about an emotion, you can create a situation that evokes the emotion in the reader.

Here are two "language environments":

Depression

You are in
a room alone with your
life scattered all over,
trying to clean up the pieces.
It feels as if it
will never get back to normal.
When you don't know
where to put something,
the mess begins to pile up.
                    — Laurie Roman (HS)

Repressed

Too many raindrops
on a small delicate
petal of a flower
seem to weigh it down
so far
as if to break it off
from itself
to fall
endlessly
limp
and
frail.

      — Jill Newman (HS)

18
Emotions

At an International Poetry Festival in Rome a few years ago, a young spectator seized the microphone and said, "I mean, you know what I feel, I mean, why can't I say something, you know, my things, my feelings, I mean, my story, you know." What we know is that this person has strong feelings; what we don't know is what they are.

Few writers would want to write if they could not use their emotions, and few readers would read poems and stories devoid of feeling. F. Scott Fitzgerald said, "I must start with an emotion" and Wordsworth described "the spontaneous overflow of powerful feelings" as a source of his poetry. A story or poem might be inspired by strong feelings toward a person or situation, or by vague and undefinable feelings.

We might start writing to express one emotion, but wind up with another feeling: a journal entry can metamorphose feelings of anger into feelings of compassion, or vice versa. Inchoate feelings may bloom: a "like" poem can turn into a "love" poem. Sometimes, writing about a troublesome emotion will deactivate that feeling, just as kicking a wall dissipates frustration (and you can do it in writing without stubbing your toe). This piece of exploratory writing by a sixth grader named Dara gives us a glimpse into how writing can lead to emotional resolution:

> When I am depressed I feel like, like, like (gets higher and higher) I can't say it. OK — (sniffle), like burning my favorite teddy, and burning myself too. Then I would feel like kissing the ashes of me and my teddy and letting them blow in the wind, cause I feel better.

For the beginning writer in particular, the coming to terms with and expression of emotions are often the most enticing lures of writing. A root meaning of *emotion* is "migration" or "moving out"; a sheet of paper is an ideal place for feelings to migrate to. No matter what other concerns a writer has, emotions provide a gravitational pull to the notebook or typewriter.

•

We all share a similar emotional terrain, but the peaks and valleys vary, not only from person to person but within each individual as well. What makes *you* sad may make *me* angry; the way *you* experience and express your happiness may differ greatly from the way *I* do; and what hurts me today may amuse me tomorrow. Such emotions as sadness, anger, and happiness form a common bond among people, but if the written presentation is too common there will be no bond with the reader. Each time you write about an emotion, you *define* the emotion for that particular occasion.

Writers translate emotions into language, trying to find words that will convey the same power as a sob, giggle, or hug, and bring a tear, smile, or sigh to the reader. One method is to use concrete language and stay away from abstractions, a concept that is ingrained in Chinese poetry. Charles Reznikoff quotes an 11th-century Chinese poet who said, "Poetry presents the thing in order to convey the feeling. It should be precise about the thing and reticent about the feeling."

Writers should focus on the specific causes of emotions and the responses — internal and external — they provoke. A poem about an emotional response should contain a direct presentation of the situation that triggered the response — or an equivalent situation that could provoke such a response — and/or a palpable description of the response, perhaps using metaphor.

As Phillip Lopate points out in *Being With Children,* an ineffective way to get students to write about their feelings is to assign the topic "My Feelings," which invites generalized wishy-washy writing. Here are two approaches; the first one relies on the use of comparisons.

Emotional Comparisons

First, call for "feeling-words" and write them on the board; one list might look like this: "sad, angry, lonely, happy, shy, bewildered, love, hate, stupid, scared, blue, jealous, nervous, embarrassed, frustrated, disgusted, bitter, tired, bored, depressed, exhilarated, excited." Then improvise a poem using some of the words:

> I am sad, so sad
> because this is such a lonely day,
> a day of sad boredom
> and it gets me so angry
> because I used to be happy and exhilarated,

59

but then stupid things happened
that scared me and made me blue.
Oh, if I could get excited again
I wouldn't be sad, so sad. . . .

Pretty dull. The poem is replete with feeling-words, but devoid of feelings. The reader has no idea what it's really talking about and no reason to care. The language is too general. Now, ask the students to pick one or more feeling-words and define them through comparisons. Students can do a few short poems, using different feelings, or write several images for a single feeling. Another possibility is to make an *emotion chain,* in which emotion-definitions segue into each other. The language should be as physical and visual as possible.

When I feel lonely
I feel like I have band-aids
all over my body.

When I'm mad
it's like trying to
take your reflection out of the water.

When I feel funny
it is like I'm a clown
doing a handstand
on my nose.

When I am scared,
I feel like someone
is grabbing my feet.

When I am lonely
I feel like a cereal
that's only taken out at breakfast
not even every day.

When I am sad
I am like a raindrop
hitting an umbrella.
— Various Students (E)

Being frustrated is like
being locked in a two by two
room with a grandmother
while listening to Lawrence Welk
and having a sick dog
sit on your lap
for eternity.

60

When I am happy I feel like ✗
a beautiful girl
is dragging me
away in a laundry bag
while I'm asleep.
                    — Peter Orthodoxn (HS)

When disgusted ✗
I feel like chalk pressing
and crushing upon a huge board
leaving behind its contents
dead and lifeless,
severed in two pieces
like A&P ground beef
under the buns of a
doublemeat cheeseburger
enclosed in an envelope
to be mailed to nowhere
forever.
                    — Mike Maloney (HS)

Emotions as Conditions

This assignment emphasizes all facets of an emotion. *Think of an emotion as a physical condition (for example, the common cold) which can be broken down into the following facets: causes, symptoms, and reactions:*

CONDITION: common cold.

CAUSES: I went out without my coat; I stood in line in the rain; I haven't been getting enough sleep; I haven't been eating well; I kissed someone who has a cold.

SYMPTOMS: My throat is scratchy; my eyes are watery; I am sniffling; my body feels weak; I have a fever.

REACTIONS: I drink a lot of fluids, rest as much as I can, and wait until it goes away.

Now, do the same thing with an emotion, breaking it down into the following: factors that can precipitate the feeling; the way it feels (you can use imagery, as you did in the previous assignment); and what you might do in reaction to the emotion, either as a treatment ("When I am lonely I call my friends,") or as a way of acting it out, as in the Feelings: Do Something assignment ("When I am in love I smile and stare at the other person.")

CONDITION: Embarrassed.

SYMPTOMS: Face turns red and feels hot; lump in the throat; arms feel shaky; stomach feels quivery; legs feel stiff.

61

CAUSE: Saying something you shouldn't have; pants falling down; tripping when you are trying to show off; someone yelling at you; getting someone else in trouble.

REACTION: Run away; lock yourself in your room forever; talk to a friend who didn't see it; talk to your parents about it.
— Miriam Liss (E)

A variation is for students to write about the symptoms of an emotion without naming it, and see if the other students can guess what the emotion is:

Bored

I don't feel like watching television.
Nothing's good in the movies.
I'm looking in a dark room,
or hitch hiking for a hundred years.
Or staring at somebody's head for 24 hours.
Drawing the same thing for 64 hours.
More like having to stay in bed all day,
or stuck up in the hospital for a week
without any visitors.
— Jordan Jones (E)

A session can be devoted to a single emotion, such as anger, using all the approaches thus far (Feelings: Do Something; Language Environment; Emotional Comparisons; and Emotions As Conditions). If you use *anger,* point out that *mad* also means *crazy,* and discuss what causes people to get crazed with anger sometimes. What makes the students angry at home, in the street, or in the classroom? What makes teachers and parents angry? How do various people experience and express anger?

19
Communication

Billions of words have been written from "I" to "you," with readers invited to eavesdrop, ears pressed against the paper walls. Writers often communicate to a specific person; high school students and I came up with these reasons one would put it in writing rather than just talk to the person:

1) You have something complicated to say and don't think you can just "say it"—it must be thought out carefully.

2) You want to get it all out without interruption—it is frustrating when you start to vent your spleen and, while your spleen is venting, the person replies, "Say no more, you're absolutely right" or covers his or her ears and hums.

3) You are too embarrassed to say it face to face.

4) You want a permanent record of your thoughts.

5) Your communication with this person is only a departure point; you want the literary license to alter some feelings and facts.

6) You *want* other people to eavesdrop, for your words to have a wider audience.

We then discussed possible reasons for not even showing an "I/You" piece to the "You": Perhaps one is really talking to oneself, and the act of writing is sufficient. Or, one student reported, she "once wrote a poem to a boy but by the time I was finished and ready to show it to him I had realized what a jerk he was and that he didn't deserve it." (At least she got a poem out of the situation.) Another student responded that sometimes she's too shy to let the other person know how she's really feeling.

One of the pitfalls of sharing "I/You" poems is the possibility of inadequate feedback. One student said, "You write something to someone you feel strongly about; there are tears in your eyes as you are writing and you can't wait to show it to him, and he responds, 'Oh, that's nice,' and then changes the subject to, 'Did you go to the store today?'"

It's possible that this recipient was extremely moved by the poem but was unable to express his reaction. Perhaps he could have best responded with his own poem (the Japanese tradition of 'reply poems' is one we should import). Don't ever take someone's reaction at face value, for the expression on that face might not accurately reflect what is going on behind it. The person might be distracted at the time, or might not even grasp the significance of the poem. One of the advantages of writing is that a poem will withstand, and possibly be enhanced by, the intervention of time. A friend wrote a poem for me in college, which I recently discovered and was more moved by than when I originally read it, when I probably responded by saying, "That's nice. Say, did you go to class this morning?"

I tell students that any benefits writers get from other people—compliments, publication, or, for the few, fame and fortune—have to be considered extras. Delightful extras, to be sure, but not to be counted upon. I'm not saying you should pretend that you don't care what others think—almost every writer does—but try to make the act of writing its own reward.

Here is a poem of great intimacy, private words addressed in public. (The poet may be exaggerating his own behavior for poetic effect, or writing about behavior observed in others.)

This Is a Poem to My Son Peter

this is a poem to my son Peter
whom I have hurt a thousand times
whose large and vulnerable eyes
have glazed in pain at my ragings
thin wrists and fingers hung
boneless in despair, pale freckled back
bent in defeat, pillow soaked
by my failure to understand.
I have scarred through weakness
and impatience your frail confidence forever
because when I needed to strike
you were there to be hurt and because
I thought you knew
you were beautiful and fair
your bright eyes and hair
but now I see that no one knows that
about himself, but must be told
and retold until it takes hold
because I think anything can be killed
after awhile, especially beauty
so I write this for life, for love, for
you, my oldest son Peter, age 10,
going on 11.
                              —Peter Meinke

64

Ask students for examples of how Meinke uses visual language, and point out the optimism of the last line, which intimates a change in the future.

Sometimes *what* we write to a person is less important than the *act* of communicating. As the Beatles sing in "Julia": "Half of what I say is meaningless, but I say it just to reach you. . . ."

Write an "I/You" poem. (It can be a poem you would like someone to write to you.) The only requirement is that the characters of the poem be that popular couple, "I" and "you." You might want to write it in the form of a letter.

Dear You,

I never told you this before but I always liked when you used to come to my room and talk to me, and I told you how my day at school was. I would start talking about our stepmother because I hated her so much that sometimes I felt like getting her hair and ripping it all away from her head, then knocking all her false teeth out. I used to curse her behind her back because I hated her beyond all imagination.

What I hated most was when she picked on me. That's when I really got red as a tomato and went to my room to cry. But the last time she did that I decided to run away. I ran away when I was at school so nobody would see me. I told you, wanted you to come with me since I trusted you and I knew you wouldn't tell on me, but you didn't believe I would run away. But now I'm living with Mom and you are still suffering with your stepmother. You can tell Dad to bring you on weekends and we can discuss things. I really miss you a lot. But I guess I can manage without our little talks. I hope you will be coming next week because I'm expecting you.

Sincerely yours,
Your best friend
Anonymous (E)

•

Writing Notes

Novelist and journalist Phyllis Raphael told me that some of the most important and engaging writing she does is in the form of notes, often to her children. She might write a note because she is angry that her daughter was late for school thirty-six times; to accompany a birthday gift; or to apologize for angrily saying some things she didn't mean. She says, "The act of putting myself on the page is what counts. . . I think the reason I enjoy note writing so much is because it's a form of direct communication, and there's no pressure to 'succeed' on a literary level." Basically, Raphael's approach is to "work hard to communicate what I feel as clearly and as simply as I can. . . . I value brevity. I edit myself to the bone." Sometimes she writes notes that she doesn't send, such as one particularly angry note, which "was good for me to write, but sending it wouldn't have been good for either of us." This is one she did deliver:

> Dear Julie poolie poopy droopy snoopy poopy doops,
> Please read this carefully.
> If you continue to be late to school another thirty-six times this year I will have to get tough with you.
> First of all in getting tough with you I will take the following steps.
> I will take thirty-six dollars from your allowance.
> I will say no thirty-six times when you ask me for something.
> I will smack your hand thirty-six times when you reach for a cookie.
> I will send Sweet William [Julie's horse] a letter telling him that you are the kind of person who has been late thirty-six times to school. I will take away all your privileges like smelling like a horse in this house and in the presence of Billy and me. I will ban horse smell from this house forever which means you will have to sleep in the hall.
> Getting letters like this telling me you have been late thirty-six times is a drag. When I get them I have to open them and read them and that takes valuable time from my day. I don't have time to read things like this. I'm a busy person.
> Get on the stick Julie. There are 42 days left to this term. I expect you to be on time every single one of them.

Write notes arising from situations at home or in school. You might want to share these only with the people they are directed to, or keep them to yourself.
Product is not the objective here; this activity exposes students to a way that language can be used throughout one's life, whether one becomes a writer or not. High school student Doreen Murphy finds note writing to be effective when she has "something to tell someone but I can't say it to their face. I would write it down and plant it somewhere I know they will see it. It works, too, with anyone – friends and family."

•

Talking to Oneself
Most people talk to themselves. One of the distinctions between "crazy" and "sane" people is that the crazies are less discreet about it. They talk to themselves out loud in public, while sane people either do it silently or when they're alone, often with a dog or cat providing a set of ears; or they do it in their poetry. This is a poem of inner conflict by David Ignatow:

Self-Employed

I stand and listen, head bowed,
to my inner complaint.
Persons passing by think

66

I am searching for a lost coin.
You're fired, I yell inside
after an especially bad episode.
I'm letting you go without notice
or terminal pay. You just lost
another chance to make good.
But then I watch myself standing at the exit,
depressed and about to leave,
and wave myself back in wearily,
for who else could I get in my place
to do the job in dark, airless conditions?

In "In a Dream," Ignatow adds the twist of talking to his "self" at an earlier age:

In a Dream   ʋ

at fifty I approach myself,
eighteen years of age,
seated despondently on the concrete steps
of my father's house,
wishing to be gone from there
into my own life,
and I tell my young self,
Nothing will turn out right,
you'll want to revenge yourself,
on those close to you especially,
and they will want to die,
of shock and grief. You will fall
to pleading and tears of self-pity,
filled with yourself, a passionate stranger.
My eighteen-year-old self stands up
from the concrete steps and says,
Go to hell,
and I walk off.

Write a poem that includes talking to yourself—complaining, praising, informing, cajoling, etc. Or, write a poem in which you talk to yourself at an earlier, or later, age.

20
Invention

Anything can happen in a poem or story; you can go as far as your imagination will take you. Some writers have resigned themselves to the notion that "I am simply not inventive." I don't accept that; a writer may *choose* to stay within the limits of day-to-day reality, but not because he or she is incapable of being inventive. The painter Courbet preferred to stick to objective reality, explaining, "Show me an angel, and I'll paint it for you." For many painters and writers, though, one of the appeals of art is that it enables you to invent what can't be seen: why limit yourself to reinventing the wheel when you can invent an angel?

The assignments in this section acquaint students with their inventive resources and how to tap them, opening up vistas of travel down the stream of consciousness. Eventually, the oars we provide them with can be replaced by their own.

•

It is possible to describe the impossible, as Kafka did when he wrote, "As Gregor Samsa awoke one morning from uneasy dreams he found himself transformed in his bed into a gigantic insect," one of the most famous imaginative leaps in literary history. Simply by arranging words on a page, a writer can make a clerk become a roach or make trees dance on a cloud. What power—it seems a shame not to use it occasionally.

All people are surrealists when they dream; if our unconsious can create striking imagery and strange, compelling happenings while we are asleep, this fertile hotbed can also work for us during waking hours. About art that springs from the unconscious, Jung said, "We would expect a strangeness of form and content, thoughts that can only be apprehended intuitively, a language pregnant with meanings, and images that are true symbols because they are the best possible expressions for something unknown — bridges thrown out towards an unseen shore."

Juxtaposition

Surrealists shake up the rational world. Things don't always appear where they belong, or in "correct" proportion. Such tampering can have an illuminating effect. If you take a walk in the forest, you might not notice any given tree; but if you came home one night and found a tree in your living room, you'd see it like you never have before. Juxtaposition — a staple of inventive writing — relies on *placement* rather than the creation of something new (as most inventions rely on the juxtaposition of already existing components). If one were to do a painting of the Queen Elizabeth ocean liner moving down Broadway with buses and cars, the viewer would be familiar with each of the elements, but the juxtaposition would be new.

Here is a poem by Gregory Corso that juxtaposes former baseball star Ted Williams with the Eiffel Tower:

Dream of a Baseball Star

I dreamed of Ted Williams

leaning at night
against the Eiffel Tower, weeping.

He was in uniform
and his bat lay at his feet
— knotted and twiggy.

"Randall Jarrell says you're a poet!" I cried.
"So do I! I say you're a poet!"

He picked up his bat with blown hands;
stood there astraddle as he would in the batter's box,
and laughed! flinging his schoolboy wrath
toward some invisible pitcher's mound
— waiting the pitch all the way from heaven.

It came; hundreds came! all afire!
He swung and swung and connected not one
sinker curve hook or right-down-the-middle.
A hundred strikes!
The umpire dressed in strange attire
thundered his judgement! YOU'RE OUT!
And the phantom crowd's horrific boo
dispersed the gargoyles from Notre Dame.

And I screamed in my dream:
God! throw thy merciful pitch!
Herald the crack of bats!

Hooray the sharp liner to left!
Yea the double, the triple!
Hosannah the home run!

In the following poem by Harry Greenberg, The Three Stooges —
known for their violent brand of slapstick — are juxtaposed with a solemn
personal occasion, a grandmother's funeral. This juxtaposition illuminates
The Three Stooges as human beings rather than as screen characters,
thereby making the occasion even more poignant:

The Three Stooges at My Grandmother's Funeral

The Stooges did not attend the funeral services,
but they're the first ones to the cemetery.
Moe hugs my father.
Curly walks solemnly down the row of cars
reminding the drivers to turn off their lights.
And Larry chats with my Aunt Sybil,
reminiscing about how her dog Coco
got into the habit of knocking the receiver
off its hook and barking into the phone
every time it rang.
"You know, Syb, we put that piece of business
in our tenth short, *Malice in the Palace.*

The rabbi asks my father to recite
the Mourners' Kaddish with him.
My father's voice drips from his mouth,
in a few moments tears replace his words.
He throws a handful of dirt on the coffin
and it lands in a tight clump.
Moe drops a fistful of dirt into the grave
and whispers, "This is the first time
I've ever thrown dirt at anyone
other than a Stooge. I don't like it."
He helps my father back to the limousine,
both of them weeping like tiny birds.
Larry and Curly shake hands with the rabbi.
The Stooges wave as we pull away.
From far off they flutter and shiver.

Ask the students to write a piece based on an interesting juxtaposition, as in the Corso and Greenberg poems. You might want to provide
younger students with more structure, such as the following activity.
Ask the class to name an interesting animal ("armadillo"), a job
("waiter"), and a place they've never been to ("London"). Put them together
and you have "The armadillo went to London to work as a waiter." The
children who came up with this combination got a laugh out of it, and I

pointed out how the three words separately (armadillo, waiter, London) were nothing compared to juxtaposing them in an image. By linking the words, a picture forms; but the picture is vague, so I asked, "What kind of waiter?" and one response was, "A head waiter in a fancy restaurant," while another student wanted the armadillo to be dishing out greasy french fries in a diner. Being specific sharpens the picture and makes it easier to get it even sharper: if the armadillo is working in a fancy restaurant, he might be wearing a tuxedo, whereas at the diner his attire could be a grease-stained T-shirt and blue jeans. Thus, this exercise fosters not only juxtaposition but development as well.

Once I asked for an animal, a place, and "something you do." The responses were "snake, Puerto Rico, and play": "The snake when to Puerto Rico to play." But play what? "Tennis," someone shouted, and they all had a mental picture of a snake playing tennis in Puerto Rico.

You can set up a juxtaposition (as above) or ask students to create their own. Then they should elaborate. This is what a sixth grader did with our armadillo waiter:

Arnold Armadillo

An Armadillo walks down the street
To his job in London, England
Where he works as a head waiter
He dresses in red with a white shirt and a black bow tie
With a napkin hanging on his left arm
He steps to the door and bows
With his right hand pointing to a table
Many people come to Cat's Cuisine
He is a perfect gentleman

When he gets home he rests on his back
He talks French and English very well
He loves just sitting down and watching T.V.
He eats fly souffle
He also eats snake souffle
His favorite dish is chocolate rat

His friends are Tom Cat, Petey Dog, Jerry Mouse, and Alfred Armadillo
They love visiting the Queen
The Queen loves Arnold Armadillo
She adores his cooking and service
They swim and dance disco at Afie's Bark and Young Men's and
      Women's Animal Association.
         —Nina Diaz (E)

There are endless variations to juxtaposition assignments. Once, I asked each student to write down 1) a famous person they like or admire, living or dead, real or fictional; 2) a place they have never been to, but would love to go to; 3) something exciting and/or scary they once did; 4) something

71

exciting and/or scary they have never done; 5) a famous person they hate or fear, living or dead, real or fictional.

Now, take all these ingredients and cook them up in a literary stew.

Relentless Logic

A second approach to inventive writing is to create an impossible premise and pursue it logically. This is where orderly minds shine, for when an orderly mind gets a grasp on inventive writing, watch out! Once a premise has been established, the rest of the piece can be constructed methodically. If the reader is willing to buy the wacky premise, the writer will throw in the rest for free. Kafka's *Metamorphosis,* from which I quoted earlier, is a classic example: once we have accepted that Gregor can no longer shop for his clothes in the men's department, the rest follows somewhat naturally.

Russell Edson is a master of such writing, as evidenced by this prose poem:

Antimatter

On the other side of a mirror there's an inverse world, where the insane go sane; where bones climb out of the earth and recede to the first slime of love.

And in the evening the sun is just rising.

Lovers cry because they are a day younger, and soon childhood robs them of their pleasure.

In such a world there is much sadness, which, of course, is joy...

Here are opening premises to other Russell Edson pieces. Read them to the class to give students a feel for this approach; students who can't come up with their own premises might want to borrow one of Edson's and take it from there:

A toy maker made a toy wife and a toy child.

An elephant of long service to a circus retired to a small cottage on a quiet street. . . .

We are having trouble controlling an umbrella, which has come to life.

You haven't finished your ape, said mother to father, who had monkey hair and blood on his whiskers.

There was an ugliness factory where ugliness was manufactured.

You are about to break through, like something in a shell.

A man had just married an automobile.

A dead man is introduced back into life.

A lighted window floats through the night like a piece of paper in the wind.

72

✗ A man dresses up like a judge and stands before a mirror and sentences himself. . . .

A scientist has a test tube full of sheep.

What all these premises have in common is that the rules governing the way the world works have been changed (the poet as omnipotent legislator). Each time you write such a poem or story, you create a new world, with its own laws of nature.

Premises don't have to be as clearly stated as they are in Edson's poems. Here is a poem by Bruce Weigl in which the rules for the behavior of mice have been amended.

Whistle Mouse

The mouse doesn't see me
he stretches out on the floor
peels his fur off
he begins at the feet
a pair of black leather shoes
he squirms out of more fur
he has a blue sharkskin suit
but the suit is clean and fits well
finally he pulls the mouse fur
over his head like a sweater
another mouse head
he holds up a sign
WHISTLE JACOB'S LADDER
I whistle and the mouse dances
much faster than I can whistle

Why not a dancing mouse in a sharkskin suit?

Ask students to create a premise that alters the expected, and write about it somewhat logically. If you wind up with nothing but a lot of talking animals, you might want to suggest other possibilities.

•

Exaggeration

A third approach to inventive writing is Exaggeration, in which a *realistic* opening premise is extended until it bursts through into surrealism. This poem of mine starts with an unfortunate, but possible, occurrence:

Displacement

✗ a loss poem

You come home,
find your possessions gone,

you sigh
and go to bed.

Awakening abruptly,
you find your bed gone,
stolen from under your nose.
So tired,
you go back to sleep.
You'll investigate later.

You re-awake
to a slap of chill wind.
Someone has made off with the south wall.
Back to sleep,
overcoat on blanket.

You dream
of walking off to distant places.
When you wake again
you are a double amputee.

By morning
there is no
trace of you.

When assigning inventive poems, caution students not to make a conscious effort to have a message to their madness. If a "meaning" arises, so be it, but this is a chance for them to get away from the constraint of meaningfulness. This advice goes as well for the next section, which is closely related to invention.

21
Language Poems

Occasionally I find that a poem or story will be inspired more by the sound of the words than their meaning. I follow where the words lead me. Sometimes a recognizable pattern or plot materializes, sometimes the result is nonlinear language. With some trepidation I'll refer to nonlinear pieces as "Language Poems," admitting the redundancy of that label. Language Poems use elements of surrealism—particularly a reliance on the unconscious—but tend to have less narrative development than the poems and assignments in the Invention section.

The more inscrutable Language Poems are more akin to the paintings of the Abstract Expressionists than of the Surrealists, and are impossible to paraphrase without destroying them. Some people are infuriated by them not because they don't *like* what is happening, but because they can't *figure out* what is happening. And yet these same people might admire a painting comprised of colors, shapes, images, and patterns with no discernible subject matter, citing the painting's "tremendous energy," and pointing out "the deep feeling here; look at the somber tones easing into an explosion of color." Like paint, language has texture, energy, and tone—elements that need not be linked to a narrative.

Language Poetry is not to everyone's liking, but students should have this approach as an option; for some it's an acquired taste. Here is an example of a student poem that would be impossible to paraphrase:

Stapling My Face

india ink babies crawling on my linen.
roaches disfiguring apples. smoke making my eyes sweat, lashes
      falling out.

not noticing beggars clad in chinese silks, nor the windmill drowning
    in the tide.
passing the buck. paper dolls running the casinos of vegas.
dogs barking, city. city. valentine dates and purple hearts. tell that
    to the G.I.'s
                   — Gerry Pearlberg (M)

Language Poems can be appreciated if you drop the demand that, because language is *capable* of communicating events and ideas, it *must* do so. When people say they don't understand some modern poetry, it is possible that they are expecting the poems to be accomplishing things that the poems are not attempting. Because they are unable to explicate a poem, some readers fear they are "missing the point." Some even accuse poets of deliberately obscuring the meaning, of being slave drivers who want readers to toil in the fields of language until they "get it."

Once, after I read nonlinear poems to a class, the teacher said, "Look, I think that stuff is too difficult for the students; to tell you the truth, *I* don't even understand it." I replied that there are some poems the reader should *digest* rather than understand. I don't mean to say that such poems are beyond scrutiny, but that they can be appreciated without wrapping them into neat packages of explication.

The imagery in such a poem might have private meaning to the author; the reader need not know the meaning, as long as the *power* is felt. In an interview, songwriter James Taylor spoke about the sense of "conviction" in his songs and how his imagery can reach listeners even when they don't know exactly what is going on. His hit song "Fire and Rain" refers to "flying machines in pieces on the ground"; how many people who appreciate the song know that Taylor was once in a rock group called The Flying Machine?

When the writer connects with his or her material, it is likely that the reader will feel that connection. Here's a poem by high school student Yan Yan Lau:

A butterfly flew but it didn't meet the air.
Who is at fault? Maybe next time
they will say hello.
Magic marble and shiny pennies are all I have to hope that you'll
    understand.
Our silence is our bond but this magic
will not endure.
The secret lies in words but this breaks the magic.
Maybe they'll meet tomorrow.

I told Yan Yan that I liked and was moved by the poem, and she asked, "Do you understand it?" I replied that, in a way I did. She giggled and asked, "*How* can you understand it?" to which I said, "You're speaking a

76

language I can grasp the sense of, even if I don't know the meaning of each phrase. You communicate something I can feel, not something I need to analyze. I can apply it to situations I've been in, which may be different from the particular situation you are writing about, if you *are* writing about a specific situation." At this point, a friend of Yan Yan's said, "That's what's so great about it. I know what's going on in her life so I can appreciate it on that level, too, but it has something for everyone."

In Yan Yan's case, she knew where the language was coming from, but often the references are mystifying even to the writer. A former student of mine found himself writing Language Poems that baffled him. He called me late one summer evening and told me that he had been "writing all these poems late at night and they kind of scare me" because they "write themselves." I assured him that there are many poets who would be happy to trade places with him. This is one of the poems:

The Hunters of the World

The hunters of the world
have gathered in an underground tavern;
At the sign of the red eagle.

Above them,
    the mountains
        (angry blisters of solid pus)
            flowed freely over
Tuesday's garbage,
and Monday's newspapers:
Pricked by a gaseous pin.

Men on Pluto invented the wheel
The ocean parroted
    the sound of the wind on wood,
    and a curious noise escaped
        the sun as
            water
                took the place of
                    centuries;
at the sign of the red eagle.
                        —Mike Eisenberg (HS)

The beauty of Language Poetry is partly in its mystery, its use of language to arouse wonder or curiosity in the reader. Such writing is not easy to do well; Language Poems have to draw the reader in. Hemingway said of some paintings that he did not like, "I did not understand them but they did not have any mystery," implying that if the paintings had mystery, it wouldn't have mattered that he didn't "understand" them.

Many people believe that the unconscious does not operate randomly, that there is an inherent, albeit elusive, order even in the most disjointed

77

poems, and writers should step out of the way when composing and let the unconscious do its job. Perhaps the most balanced way of looking at it is expressed in Max Jacob's phrase "unconscious under supervision." As supervisors, writers sift through and order the natural resources excavated from the unconscious. Language Poems that appear to have been composed spontaneously may actually have gone through many revisions.

See if the students can appreciate the mystery and wonder in the following three poems. Ask them to try to absorb the words through their skin rather than figure them out with their minds. The first one contains some mysterious goings-on, and closes on a note of wonder:

Poem

Language was almost impossible in those days
as we know it now and then.

When you tell me about your operation
I hear you, but I don't hear you.

Wind gathers behind a barn:
torches are lit, men whisper.

One wears a hat and is very serious
About the war in his bedroom.

"Does it seem like I am sleeping all the time?"
Ask me another question.

Look, Ma, I found something beautiful today
out in the forest, it's still alive. . . .
        — James Tate

Sleep

We brush the other, invisible moon.
Its caves come out and carry us inside.
        — Bill Knott

Poem

At your light side trees shy
A kneeling enters them
        — Bill Knott

Part of the impact of poems like these derives from language that reverberates. After I read "Sleep" to a sixth grade class, we discussed the use of the word "cave" and I asked the students for words they associated with caves. On one hand we had "cold, scary, dark, bats," and on the other hand we had "warmth, protection, shelter." Words like "cave" increase the reader's involvement with a poem.

This haunting poem by Wendy Salinger should be read slowly:

Time in the Body and the Time of the Body

I think the buried beat at the dirt.
Violent hallucinations of azalea burst
over the gravestones. In the very dark
of a friend of mine, a spine
formed and bloomed.

When I first read this poem, I appreciated it for its evocative language. The last sentence is a stunning, life-affirming image, but I didn't realize — until the author told me — that it is a literal reference to a pregnancy. My task in this chapter is not to make a definitive statement about the role of "meaning" in poetry, but to encourage you and your students to spend some time writing and enjoying poetry *primarily* on the basis of language.

After reading and discussing such poetry with students for about 20 minutes, ask them to write a Language Poem, using private references and/or unconscious associations. Here are three samples:

The Heroes That Once Were

They go to the cathedral where
they face the truth of their dreams,
for the truth may catch
up with the heroes they once were
and may never be again.
          — Jeannine Budihas (E)

   The wall so deep
as if to put your hand in and it drowns
   in wonder inside but never
can get out, everlasting wondering.
           — Lisa Bracero (E)

I won't deny devotion,
even with a teaspoon of despair:
but when the sky fell
I could hear a pin drop —
like a thunderless cloud rolling over
— just a tingle of a rumble.
The crash was smooth,
like a mutual surrender
provoked by consequences
and occurring before the stars began to flirt with the crescent moon.
          — Jocelyn Siegel (HS)

•

79

Verbal Cut-Ups

It doesn't happen often, but sometimes it seems like the air is sprinkled with words, and all the writer has to do is transfer them to the paper. One way to elicit Language Poems is literally to put words out in the air for everyone's plucking.

Take an anthology of poetry and tell the class you will be flipping through the pages, reading aloud a word here, a phrase there. Although you will be reading slowly, it will be much too fast for them to copy down verbatim what you say. They should write steadily as you read; about half of what they write should be excerpted from what you are saying (or what they *think* you are saying) and the other half should be their own words (which could be triggered by what you are saying). Students can combine the beginning of one spoken phrase with part of a subsequent phrase. For example, if you say, "I walked into a store. . . The rocket landed on the moon," a student might write, "I walked into the moon," or, due to mishearing, "I walked into the socket," which he or she could follow with a few words of his or her choosing before listening to you again.

After about ten minutes of this, each student has a page filled with strange images, odd combinations of words, and gibberish. Now it's time for "supervision." Students should use some of this raw material in a poem. Making linear sense is not a priority, but if a narrative does develop, that's fine. Each student is the master of his or her raw material, and may alter, delete, and add at will. The final version may contain merely a phrase or two from the raw material, or it may be a slight refinement of the first draft.

Have several students read theirs out loud. Although everyone started with the same input, the final products will vary greatly. Here is a student's raw material and revised version:

> You can not weep. I say you're a poet. Black leaves kept forgetting I once wrote a letter. My life is blue leaves behind my eyes. In the river sparks. MaMa show her son the extension key. I am not a little boy. I keep forgetting without anyone. Good morning how do the gray heroes moving back. I reach for the sky someone shakes their hands. After night we all sound like wind bags. I have to. Mad street with a picture on the wall. Blue leaves are on me.

•

> My life is blue leaves
> behind my eyes. I am not a
> little boy nor a
> hero. I always forget without
> anyone telling me.
> I walk on streets, the streets
> look like mad pictures
> because people walk on them.

At night I keep a candle
near me. In the morning I
reach for the sky. But
I still think my life is blue
leaves behind my eyes.

— Victor Carusi (E)

PART FOUR

A CATALOGUE OF
ASSIGNMENTS

22
Freewriting

Write without pausing for three minutes. If stuck for something to say, you can write "I'm stuck" or describe what is going on around you, such as "The clock just ticked, Margaret is looking at the ceiling, my foot itches." Write anything, just keep going. When time is up, give students a few minutes either to continue writing or to make legible what they have written (but no crossing out permitted).

Nonstop writing has been variously called freewriting, automatic writing, stream of consciousness, and brainstorming. I recommend three minutes as a minimum, with subsequent increases in duration. Freewriting can be used as a loosening up exercise to get the writing juices flowing, or as the basis for an entire session. Usually, *something* interesting happens; there are many things buzzing around in our minds waiting to seize our attention.

Tell students that nonsense writing is fine. In doing the following freewriting, a fourth grader had her first terrific experience with language. Lisa had previously been a reluctant, laborious writer, but my assurance that freewriting was a chance for her to let language flow without censor or censure led to a surprise party of words. Lisa's excitement grew when she heard the enthusiastic response of her classmates as I read the piece out loud.

> Yaa Yaa you you yourself something is
> making no sense I am me the real true
> me something is making me do it Yaa
> black pudding make it stop make me write
> me I you am I doing yourself is it making
> me laugh I am doing the same thing I was
> laughing about before yourself is tell-
> ing you you're making no sense nothing

will make me stop are you thinking or
writing blah yourself help, help, help
the pleasant things come nothing is
coming out the way it was supposed to
be are you listening are you talking
are you being silly make it rain make
it snow are you singing being happy
sad or silly have yourself a party
something is bad something is sad
someone is screaming something is yelling you are laughing crying shouting
being a nut I am being like you we are
doing some baking I am baking a mashed
potato pie, thick orange soup, apple
nut cakes, mushy lemon juice You are
going crazy making noise not being
yourself come sing come ring be something that you are not You hear the
ringing of a bell the howling of a dog
the singing of a chorus mooing of the
cows are you being yourself making no
sense is fun you are funny you are
laughing we are laughing together make
me stop have you seen your doctor lately
or your dentist nothing will make me go
you're talking to yourself making a
Yaa Yaa Yee Yeetime have a good time
in Dixieland so long big boy have a bad
day have a good day be no one you've
ever been My paper is coming to the
bottom I can't write anymore I am thru.
                    — Lisa Neitz (E)

Freewriting often results in a hodgepodge of seemingly unrelated words, but there is no rule that says freewriting must be disjointed. Many students have freewritten first drafts of straightforward narratives, though I ask that they *follow* the language rather than lead it, a hard concept for some students to grasp.

I've heard freewriting described as writing "off the top of your head," but it may be more accurate to think of it as allowing words to emerge from deep down. Some freewriting exercises start out vaguely and evolve into a topic that otherwise might not have occurred to the writer, such as in this sample:

I am confused. I am being hounded by things I don't understand. My mind is tired. I am going to go somewhere I don't know where. If I were able to stop the world I would pull off the people who tease and fight and pick on innocent people. I remember when my grandmother was alive. She was the sweetest person in the world. She was 57 and didn't look like she was over 40.

86

I saw a picture a few days ago and suddenly didn't know why I was so fascinated by it. It was a young girl very beautiful and graceful. I later learned it was my grandmother.

—Anne Strano (E)

Anne didn't start writing with her grandmother on the tip of her pencil. She could pursue this material by describing the photograph and giving examples of what made her grandmother so sweet. Such writing, spurred by self-probing, tends to be more authentic than pieces instigated by such instructions as "Children, this is Grandparents' Day, and I want each of you to write something about a grandparent." Through freewriting, Anne discovered that she had a real need to write about her grandmother.

In this freewriting exercise, a sixth grade boy deals with his feelings about girls:

Oh what am I doing going crazy
out of my mind I feel dizzy away
from everyone except girls all
kinds of girls. Girls whose shapes
I like or love, and girls whose shapes
I hate. Girls with terrible faces and
beautiful shapes, girls with terrible shapes
and beautiful faces.

Oh what am I doing—
judging somebody
and letting my opinion praise some
and embarrass others.

Just dreaming off into a world of beauty
or a world of crazy,
oh must I judge?
Or look and listen and learn
to know this is my reason
for writing this.

—John Tshibula (E)

The following freewriting exercise by a high school student starts with a description of the process itself, and arrives at an insight on what it means to be a child:

I am sitting here trying to decide what to write. Alan has said write whatever comes just don't stop so that is what I am doing. If I come to a stop I will fill the gap with sounds but I cannot stop. I once read that the cow jumped over the moon I wonder how he got up there. Nursery rhymes are so silly I believed them when I was young. When you are young you will believe anything — everything. That is the magic of being young I miss it.

—Carolyn Kintisch (HS)

And in this example, writing about writing and paying attention to her surroundings led a fifth grader to an allegorical vignette:

> When I write I like to write about the things I think of. The kind of things that just pop right into my head. Right now I'm thinking of the trees in the park across the street. One of them was, is shaking because the wind is blowing hard and a little girl comes over to the tree and leans against it, as if to say that she will stop it from shaking as the wind hits it with hard blows. But the tree knows that the little girl cannot stop the wind from shaking it. And so the tree keeps on shaking and the little girl runs away.
>
> —Christine Mitsis (E)

23
Notebooks

F. Scott Fitzgerald referred in "Afternoon of an Author" to the "leather-bound wastebasket which I fatuously refer to as my 'notebook.'" He was being harsh on his notebook and himself; Fitzgerald's notebooks make for better reading than the polished works of many authors.

In *The Writing Workshop: Volume I,* I discussed the value of the writer's notebook. The best feature of the notebook is that it belongs to the student, who determines its content. Unfortunately, many students are not accustomed to keeping a notebook. You might want to impose some benign coercion. When I was a college freshman, my English professor required that we write in our notebooks three times a week. Although I grumbled at what I perceived to be forced introspection, my freshman year — thanks to him — is my only year in college thus chronicled. You can do likewise and require that students make at least two notebook entries per week, suggesting that an occasional entry be about the writing workshop and/or the student's writing process.

I gave myself a more stringent assignment a few years ago. I bought a small appointment book and assigned myself to write something in it each day. Since the maximum space was small, on many days I wanted to write more than I had room for. The next year, confidence bursting, I got a large appointment book and vowed to fill each page. But my confidence had burst the seams of my discipline, and my last entry was January 16th. I've since found a medium-sized book, which I've kept faithfully for two years; on some days I jot down key phrases to be filled in later.

•

The vignette (a literary sketch — a slice-of-life) is an ideal form for notebook entries because it is short and consolidates description, narration, and perhaps dialogue. We often witness or participate in interesting scenes that can be captured in notebook vignettes and subsequently be refined or expanded.

> A very small boy carrying a cardboard tray of six large sodas walked out of McDonald's. He moved his feet slowly and carefully and never took his eyes off the sodas. In the parking lot, a man sat in a car and stared. He began tapping his fingers and couldn't sit in the same position for long. While the little boy's feet were moving more slowly, the man in the car took a long, deep breath, and then lit a cigarette. The little boy lost his balance as he stepped down into the parking lot; he stuck his tongue out the side of his mouth, but it didn't help. He tripped and spilled all of the soda. The man looked up, got out of the car, and slammed the door shut. The boy started to cry.
>
> —Christine Basile (HS)

There is a cumulative effect of vignettes that take place in the same location and/or involve the same or similar characters or situations. A short story (such as Donald Barthelme's "Robert Kennedy Saved From Drowning") or a novel (such as Renata Adler's *Speedboat*) can be built with vignettes. A series of vignettes can be a long-term project for ambitious students, who can store the raw material in their notebooks.

Alexis Deveaux's *Spirits in the Streets* uses vignettes to chronicle growing up in Harlem:

> Holding a book in her arm and a pencil resting in her hair, Michelle had an attitude the first time I noticed her. She was not interested in conversation. Her eyes dashed up and down the block in search of other words to listen to. JoJo cruised away. I walked to 8th avenue.
>
> •
>
> It is hot. Funky hot. Smells of the weekend pour from torn buildings and spread like spider nests in the air . . .
>
> •
>
> Outside, 114 street begins to dance. At 2:00 in the afternoon a dry sun melts hot buildings in the pavement. Above, the green gnats buzz and play tag around sweaty heads of little people. A volleyball game stops to let a car go by. Young ones squat on a large white square. Soda tops filled with bubble gum and wax sail from box to box on the street's skin.
>
> •
>
> 5:30. Late afternoon spreads herself like a quiet blanket over 114 street. There are a few people outside. The stoops are sparsely crowded with kids playing, women standing around and workers coming home from the job. The jukebox in the Candystore screams the melodies of James Brown. 11 young dudes play touchfootball near by. In between plays the quarterback stops to dance.

24
Visualization

Writing from observation helps train the writer's eye. The inner eye, or, as Shakespeare called it, "the mind's eye," is also an important sense for starting and developing poems and stories.

First, make sure that the students understand the concept of the inner eye by asking them to visualize something familiar, such as their bedroom or a parent. Now, tell them that you're going to say a phrase, which you want them to concentrate on, letting a mental picture develop. Although everyone starts with the same generalization, the pictures will vary.

I said "rainy day" to one class, then asked for an initial "flash," be it an overall picture or a detail. One detail response was "yellow rubber raincoat," while another student saw "raindrops dripping down a closed window against a grey background." Other responses were: "a card table in a bedroom with a chess game set up," "a puddle," "swimming in a pool in the rain," and "licking the rain."

I told the students to let their pictures grow. I asked the boy who saw a puddle if he could see anything else, and he responded, "A reflection in the puddle." Of course I asked whose reflection it was, and, without missing a beat, he responded, "God's."

"Who is in the yellow rubber raincoat?" I asked the first student, and she saw herself in the woods, coming upon a rabbit. I told the other students to do likewise with their pictures. When they had scenes they could grasp, it was time for writing. If they saw a "still life," they could animate the picture with narrative. Here's the first draft of the "yellow raincoat" response:

> When I think of a rainy day I imagine myself walking deep into the woods with a yellow raincoat, a big brown umbrella, and black boots. I picture a rabbit under a tree, a baby deer walking along the path. And then I

91

picture a lonely puppy lost and I hear his cries. Then I pick him up and wrap him in a blanket and I walk deeper into the woods. I see two little birds under a mushroom. I walk deeper and then the rain stops and I can smell the fresh fragrance of the trees and flowers. I see an owl and I climb up the rough tree....

—Lisa Bracero (E)

As it stands now, this piece of writing is an exercise in visualization, but it has the makings of a story. In the process of revising, the words that stem from the original exercise should be nipped out, leaving

On a rainy day I walk deep into the woods with a yellow raincoat, a brown umbrella, and black boots, I see a rabbit under a tree....

For this to become a story, something would have to *happen* — probably with the dog — and Lisa would have to develop her persona: who is this person walking in the woods on a rainy day? This episode doesn't have to be used as the beginning of a story. Weeks later, Lisa could find herself writing a story about a girl who runs away from home. Unable to decide what to write next, Lisa might incorporate this fragment. (Fragments in the folder are like money in the bank.)

Open Visualization

Have a student close his or her eyes and let a picture emerge without an outside suggestion. When a picture emerges, the student describes it to the rest of the group, and then other students ask questions that help fill in the picture or advance it to the next frame. A full-scale story can emerge from this activity, which can be done in small groups, with students taking turns visualizing.

One student opened with the picture "writing on a train." Questions included, "Where is the train going?" "Who else is on it?" "Look closely at the paper — what are you writing?" "You get off the train — who is there to meet you?" "What do you do with what you wrote?" This can be an exciting and productive way to develop material. Students may not literally "see" all their responses, which may result more from language than from visualization, but the visual component should be emphasized.

Another way of approaching visualization, especially with lower elementary grades, is to ask students: "You are walking in a dream and you turn a corner; what do you see?" Or, "You reach a door that says only *you* may open it. Open it. What do you see?"

92

25
Gesture and Movement

As any actor can tell you, language is only one means of communication; we also speak with gestures and movements. Sometimes body language reinforces spoken words (as when "I love you" is said while an open hand gently brushes against a cheek), but gesture and movement can also play *against* words (as when "I love you" is said with fingers crossed behind the back).

As any mime or dancer can show you, there need not be any words at all to get something across. One of my classes went to see the Alvin Ailey Dancers — the first time most of them had ever seen a dance performance — and when I asked the students what impressed them the most, one answered, "They didn't *say* anything."

"Not with words they didn't," I replied, "but are you sure they didn't say anything?" The students agreed that a lot was communicated. Some students were surprised at how much the dancers communicated with their hands and other parts of their body. Dance, they discovered, is more than being good with your feet.

Incorporating movement and gesture is a valuable resource for a writer, one that is often overlooked. Students tend to use adverbs and adjectives when a gesture or movement might be more effective. For example:

"Hi, my name is Bobby," he said shyly.
"Welcome, Bobby," she responded warmly and offered her hand, which he took tentatively.

There is nothing *wrong* with this passage, but it would be stronger like this:

"Hi, my name is Bobby," he said, looking at his left foot, which was shuffling in the dirt.

"Welcome, Bobby," she responded warmly with her hand outstretched, taking a step toward him. Bobby slowly lifted his hand and moved it toward her as if checking to see if a frying pan was too hot.

Adverbs can be useful ("warmly" was left in), but students should be adept at other options.

This poem by David Ignatow uses gesture and movement to show a *lack* of communication:

Spinning

I have my hands out to you
but you say your hands
do not exist. You also say
that I do not have hands,
that I have an illusion of hands
and that speaking to you
is speaking to myself,
appealing to myself
to be at one with me.
You show me what you mean
by spinning, standing
in one place — a humming top.
It delights you
and you urge me on.
I begin to turn
as I begin to weep.

Write a scene with dialogue, exaggerating the use of gesture and movement. Don't be afraid of using too much movement; this is practice. It might make it easier if you first conceive the situation (two people in a discotheque or a fancy restaurant) and the kind of people (awkward or elegant). Or, write a scene with no words, perhaps with two people who don't speak each other's language, or two people at the library or someplace else where they must be silent.

•

Describe an observed movement, such as a police officer directing traffic or a basketball player shooting a foul shot.

•

Ask someone in the class who has studied dance or theater to do an improvisation for the other students to describe.

•

"Choreograph" with words a series of movements and gestures: instructions for an individual or group to move in whatever ways you tell them. You might want to think of this as a scene for a ballet or a movie; you do not have to stay within the realm of the physically possible.

From a deep sleep,
roll out of bed onto the floor.
Squint one eye open,
lurch forward, teetering, on one foot,
to an upright position.
Shake your head.
Walk swaying back and forth
as if drunk, reach your hand out,
grab the small, round, resounding
clock. Watch it,
as you hurl it into the beige wall.
Grin at the springs,
walk back to your bed,
fall face forward into the warmth.
Sleep peacefully.

— Laura Fisher (HS)

26
How to Spot. . .

I was on the subway going to an elementary school on Valentine's Day, wary that the kids would write poems replete with red roses, blue violets, and insulting rhymes. I tried to come up with a Valentine's Day assignment that would result in something fresh, but couldn't think of anything. I decided to read the newspaper for a couple of stops before renewing my quest.

And there, in the *Daily News,* was an idea for the taking. A feature article about a private investigator carried a sidebar headlined "How to Spot a Suspect," which contained a list of incriminating "clues," including:

Crossing and recrossing legs. . . It lessens tension on the muscular system.

Licking lips.

Verbal gestures feigning deafness. When a persons asks, "Will you repeat the question," they are stalling for time to think up an answer.

Avoiding eye contact.

When I got to school, I wrote "How to Spot a Suspect" on the board and read the list to the class, adding that these are not scientific, surefire symptoms of criminality, but merely indications that someone is nervous. Then I mentioned Valentine's Day and erased "Suspect," replacing it with "Someone in Love."

Write someone's actions and reactions when in love—with you or anyone else.

How to Spot Someone in Love with You

When they talk to you, they just say: "Yes, a ha, and okay," never "no."

When you look at the person they will turn their head and act like they weren't looking.

When they ask you, "Do you have a boyfriend?" (or girlfriend); that's always their line. That gives you the clue. If you like the person you say, "No," if you don't like them you say, "Yes." But the main thing is if they wink at you or raise their eyebrows.

When they don't care too much about what they used to care about.

When they stare at you when walking and bang their head into a pole.

When they fail all their subjects, get punished for a year, get hit by a bus, but just keep that smile.

When they're always asking stupid questions just to get some kind of conversation, like "What class are you in?" Your reply is "I'm in your class."

When you notice them out of a big crowd of all their friends they turn red as a tomato and start to giggle.

When you ask them to jump off the George Washington Bridge and they just say, "Yeah, sure, tomorrow at noon."

When they take the same bus you do even though they live the other way.

When they call you up for the homework even though you saw them copy it down.

When they keep hitting you for no reason.

> — Jadine Fotis, Deiana Pacheco, Robin Snow,
> Catherine Herbst, Nina Diaz, William Gowan (E)

How to Spot Someone in Love

Spotting someone in love is easy if you know what to look for.

If you tell him she doesn't like him,
and he says, "I don't care, I never liked her"
while he is busy biting his nails or finding
something to break,
he likes her.

If you tease him that he likes her,
and he laughs like he doesn't know
what you're talking about,
but he doesn't throw a punch at you,
he likes her.

Sometimes if you ask a boy who likes a girl
if he likes her or another girl,
he will pick the other one.

Sometimes if a boy doesn't like a girl that much,
and is talking to her,
it will be easy for him to find something to say.
But if he likes her,
he won't find anything to say.

Sometimes if there is a dance coming up,
a boy will pick any girl *but* the one
that he likes.

—Michael Bromley (E)

27
Slow Motion

"Pacing" is an important component of narrative; a writer cannot treat all actions and thought processes with the same number of words. Time must be managed strategically: a year can pass in a paragraph, followed by a 15-page dinner scene. Filmmakers use slow motion to elongate time, thereby emphasizing details. Writers don't actually slow down the action, but rather present it in more detail. As we saw in Annie Dillard's moth excerpt (see Observation), a writer can describe with intricacy and nuance an event lasting a short period of time.

For this assignment, students set their pencils for slow motion. One technique is to visualize the event, as if watching a slow motion film, and transcribe it into words.

Narrate, in the first person, an activity you do well. It can be an everyday activity like crossing the street or making breakfast, or it can be an athletic maneuver like pitching a baseball or serving in tennis. Write in the present tense and include everything, even if you think it's boring. Stretch it out. You can make deletions on the next draft.

Feeding My Dog

I pick up my dog Cindy's green bowl and put it on the kitchen table while my dog is following me everywhere I go. I get her bag of food and scoop some moist chunks and put them in her bowl while she's looking at me like I'm crazy. She then barks three times. Finally I'm finished. Cindy is so happy that she can't stop wagging her tail. I pat her on her soft head and put her green bowl on the floor next to her water bowl so she can have a drink while she is eating her delicious dinner. "Crunch, crunch, crunch!" my dog eats noisily. Now she comes to me and wipes her nose all over my pants and bed. Then I play ball with her for a long while until I have to go to bed. I kiss her goodnight and stroke her soft black hair while she licks my hands and face. I depart from Cindy sadly.

—Barbara Lewison (E)

Because the sequence of events is predetermined, this is a good assignment for students who find it difficult to structure their writing. Their command over the subject matter enables them to concentrate on language.

•

Write about a pivotal moment in your life or someone else's, stretching it out on the page; it could be someone being saved from drowning or getting bad (or good) news. Or, take a totally typical moment, such as saying goodbye before going to school in the morning, and write about it as if every single detail were crucial.

This approach can transfigure the much-maligned "How I Spent My Summer Vacation" into a viable assignment. Ask students not to tell about their whole vacation, but to pick brief incidents and write about them in slow motion.

28
Found Poems

A Found Poem is a non-literary text in which the finder has recognized an ironic or poignant quality. One becomes the "author" of a found poem by lifting the text — often an excerpt — out of its natural habitat and into the literary arena, like putting a frame around a discarded object and hanging it on a museum wall. The words are usually grouped by linebreaks; a skillful linebreaker can inject poetic energy into such non-literary prose as a memo, newspaper article, or a politician's quotes (a book of poetry was published consisting of excerpts from the Watergate tapes broken into lines).

Doing Found Poems teaches us how to recognize the poetic nature of a text, how to excerpt from it, if necessary, and how to break the lines. Charles Reznikoff's *Testimony* books are based on transcripts of court cases that Reznikoff edited by deletion and put into poetic form, making only minor changes in the text to keep the language simple and direct, as in this selection:

Amelia was just fourteen and out of the orphan asylum; at her
        first job — in the bindery, and yes sir, yes ma'am, oh, so
        anxious to please.
She stood at the table, her blonde hair hanging about her
        shoulders, "knocking up" for Mary and Sadie, the stitchers
("knocking up" is counting books and stacking them in piles
        to be taken away).
There were twenty wire-stitching machines on the floor,
        worked by a shaft that ran under the table;
as each stitcher put her work through the machine,
she threw it on the table. The books were piling up fast
and some slid to the floor

(the forelady had said, Keep the work off the floor!);
and Amelia stooped to pick up the books—
three or four had fallen under the table
between the boards nailed against the legs.
She felt her hair caught gently;
put her hand up and felt the shaft going round and round
and her hair caught on it, wound and winding around it,
until the scalp was jerked from her head,
and the blood was coming down all over her face and waist.

"Find" a poem from any non-literary source. Put it into linebreaks.

Letter in a Library

      dear Peaches,
nothings up.
yeah it was alright. thank
you happy aneversary
to you too.
fine im bored.
oh Im in a great mood.
okay. burp says you didnt do nothing
for him. yes
he still doesn't like you.
its ok about last night. I hope
you had fun at queens.
im glad that you love me. i like you to. (only kiddy) love
ya,
      Steven
               —Gerry Pearlberg (M)

29
Eavesdropping

Most children are taught that it isn't polite to eavesdrop, but special dispensation (within limits) has been granted to writers. Many "eavesdroppings" are funny or mysterious — especially when heard out of context — and can inspire stories and poems. Discretion, a quality I constantly allude to in a writing workshop, is essential for this assignment:

Passively eavesdrop for the next couple of days. Enter into your notebook any snippets of conversation that strike you. Bring the results to class.

Ask volunteers to read one or two of their eavesdroppings, giving background information if they wish. Point out the parts that capture the rhythm and poetry of speech. Occasionally focus on a particularly evocative quotation and ask students to embellish it: what if the quotation were in a story — what would be going on, and what would happen next? One student overheard a woman say to a salesclerk, "I want my clothes to *look* expensive." Why? Is there a special occasion, or does she always feel this way?

These eavesdroppings now become collective property, either of the whole class or a small group; if possible, put them on a ditto sheet. Ask the students either to write a poem or story built almost exclusively on the eavesdroppings (using their own connecting words) or to build a piece around one or two quotations.

High school student Anne Larsen overheard "He's just the pizza man, you'll never see him again in your life," a quotation that was picked up by several classmates and which inspired Anne to write "Deliveries," which ends:

What if I came to *you*
with whole ripe olives and extra mushrooms,
my palms warm from the bottom of the box?

I use two discretion ground rules for this assignment:

1) Eavesdrop only on that which is naturally available to you: don't stick your ear against a keyhole or listen to a phone call on an extension. Good places to eavesdrop without intruding are restaurants, public transportation, the street, and on line.

2) Don't use material that could hurt people or betray their confidence, even if they talked loudly enough for you to hear. It might be best to get most of your material from strangers.

This assignment develops the writer's ear — the ability to glean interesting material from the words that swirl around us. The writing part fosters skills in making transitions and developing raw material.

I've Got Pepto Bismol-Colored Walls

If you admit something, it seems to me
that's what you become, but faith kept me
back awhile. I've been working on The Simple Solution
to a Rubik's Cube. I think I'm quite done although
I have some questions before I just tear it all up.
What did the common man have intelligence for? Let's
see how they sound without anything being done to them.
I don't understand it, I'm so happy!
                                    —Kathryn Lambert (HS)

30
Mimicry

Most writers go through periods of being highly influenced by particular writers: "Oh yes, my sophomore year at college I was Faulkner, followed by a Gertrude Stein semester, a year of 19th-Century Russians, on to Dashiell Hammet, and then I lived in Paris and wrote like Dr. Seuss."

A sixth grader named Bruno Blumenfeld was reading Judy Blume books, and her influence showed up in his stories:

> When you're 13 you have a lot to worry about. Like girls for instance....At lunch the girls sit in a whole different section. Don gets his jollies by sneaking over and listening to their conversations. Today Don talked me into going over there.
> "I got my period last night."
> Not this. "Don, I'm going to throw up...."

This assignment goes beyond influence—into mimicry.

Pick a paragraph by an author you admire—perhaps one who baffles or intimidates you—and mimic it. Stay as close as possible to the "voice" and sentence structure.

In doing this exercise, students can learn how other writers tick. They also internalize concepts of grammar, punctuation, and syntax. You might want to select several models, offering students a choice or assigning them according to need. Students who have trouble writing long sentences could be given Henry James, while long-winded students could use a little Hemingway.

The author mimicked need not be a Hemingway or Henry James; sometimes it's more beneficial for a student to mimic other students. Doris, a third grader, was going through class after class with hardly any results. I gave her a couple of literary magazines from other schools and said she could mimic any of the material. For a couple of sessions, Doris virtually copied poems. Gradually, she used more of her own material, borrowing structures but copying lines verbatim only when she got stuck. Sometimes she combined elements from different poems. She was pleased with the pages she was filling, but I worried that this would become a crutch for her. However, she weaned herself from the magazines before I had to suggest that she do so.

There is even some benefit in copying a writer's work verbatim. When Joan Didion was in high school, she typed Hemingway stories "to learn how his sentences worked. I taught myself to type at the same time."

31
People

People come and go; one way to keep or regain them is to write about them. Writers can also create new people, or make amalgams of the real and the invented. Among the most satisfying experiences for a writer is to create a character who comes alive to the reader and who will be missed by writer and reader when the piece is finished.

In order for a character to be convincing, the reader must see more than the tip of the iceberg. Often, it's during the composing process that the writer gets to know the characters, which may mean that early sections need to be revised in light of later revelations.

I once wrote a poem about a "Mr. Gutman," but I didn't delineate his character well. David Ignatow, my workshop teacher, responded, "Now, if you had showed this poem to William Carlos Williams, he would have said, 'So, you *know* Mr. Gutman? Then *tell* me about him!'" Truth was, although I had invented Mr. Gutman, I didn't know him.

At a fiction workshop, Kurt Vonnegut responded to a story I was working on by asking me about the characters. His questions went beyond what was on the page, and I began to talk about them as *people* rather than as functionaries programmed to perform literary tasks. When I revised the story, the characters had more depth, even though I used only a little of the material from my conversation with Vonnegut. (Actors sometimes prepare for roles by improvising in character; these improvisations inform their performances, and some screenwriters and playwrights incorporate material from improvisations into their scripts. This approach can be used in the writing workshop, by having students do improvisations with characters from stories in progress.)

I begin class sessions on characterization with a discussion of how people are differentiated from each other. There are genetically determined physical characteristics (height, eye color); physical aspects over which we have partial control (facial expression, body shape); and physical features over which we have almost total control (clothing, hair style). People also distinguish themselves by how they act and react, what they say and how they say it, and by their quirks and habits. Some people put ketchup on almost everything they eat; others — Alfred Hitchcock for one — despise the very notion of that thick, sweet, red stuff oozing out of a bottle and onto food. Some people walk and talk in ways as distinctive as signatures. One friend of mine paces back and forth when he's on the phone, extending the wire to its limits at each end; I used this detail in a story because it seemed to fit the character I was creating, even though that character was otherwise unlike my friend.

Writers who can detect and use the above traits have a head start in developing characters who breathe. Readers should care, one way or the other, about literary characters, and it's easier to care about someone you know.

•

Physical Portraits

Describe someone's appearance, as in these excerpts from The Breaks *by Richard Price.*

> ...He had a high forehead that was so shiny pink and blemish-free that it looked boiled. That forehead, combined with phosphorescently white teeth and a short fastidious lacquered-looking jet black Jerry Lewis crop gave him a spanky-squeaky aura and made him seem like the type that would go into shock at the sight of a soiled ashtray....

> Her two front teeth were both chipped at the meeting point between them, and her eyes were permanently pulled down at the outside corners so that she looked like she was about to say "awww" or something wistful. ...Her fingernails were bitten down to the limit and her fingertips billowed over the nail line in tender pink puffed arcs.

Behavioral Self-Portraits

This assignment deals with a character you know well: yourself. Most visual artists try their hand at a self-portrait; for one thing, the model is always available and doesn't charge a fee. A Behavioral Self-Portrait, unlike the painter's, emphasizes behavior patterns and attitudes rather than physical features. Use comparisons when appropriate (a device unavailable to painters).

"Who am I?" is too large a question to deal with in a short poem, so isolate aspects of yourself by asking, "What are some of the components that, when added together, make up 'me'?" Out of all the things you could say about yourself, pick a few that reverberate.

My arms are wrapped fast around myself.
I hear my sister breathing loudly down the hall.
The Begonia is living.
Lenore is my friend.
There are cigarettes I hate on the dresser.
The door is wide open.
No one is coming in.
Steve is away, camping alone for four days.
My dog has a tumor.
My mother and father have jobs.
I don't.
I'm middle class in America.
I love my country.
I walk the streets at two a.m. nude.
No, I don't.
My older sister is married.
I will go to college and soon be an adult.
Ducks laugh in the pond at night when no one's there.
My other sister is homosexual.
I can drive a car well.
I love the black sweater in the closet.
My father gave it to me.
I am seventeen and a spy.
My body is on the chair.
I don't shave my legs.
I am a woman.
It's autumn and cold outside.
Not inside.
My hands are ripe for you.
I cry.
I hate to go to sleep.
I love dessert and the sun going down on the highway overpass.
Kiss me.
                              — Amy Smiley (HS)

Me

      Pulling Up My Sleeves:
I always seem to pull up my sleeves
hot or cold even in snow
it never fails me
I pull up my sleeves

      Putting on My Watch:
Every morning when I get up
I put on my watch
even if I'm not going anywhere
I put on my watch

Combing My Hair:
I always comb my hair
when it's neat I still comb it
twice in the morning, twice in the afternoon
and twice at night
I comb my hair

Leaning Back in My Chair:
Every time I sit down
I lean back in my chair
even in a formal place
I lean back in my chair
even at my house I do it
I lean back in my chair

I Always Want To Punch Someone:
I seem to do it
playing or not
I ask to see if they'll do it playing
and if they don't
I punch anyway
— Daniel Hano (E)

Behavioral Portraits of Others
"My Friend Chris" is a caricature, a portrait based on exaggeration:

My Friend Chris

Chris and his friends walk
into the restaurant.
He flashes his money around,
He shows off to his friends,
They try to ignore him.

We're in the restaurant,
He orders three large pizzas,
He buys ten sodas,
We sit at the biggest table,
We wait for the food.

The food comes,
It won't fit on the table,
Chris gets up and looks for another,
He finds a big one,
He sits down and tells us to bring over the food.

We finally bring the food,
We see Chris resting in his chair,
He's asleep.

We don't want to wake him,
but a strong force pulls us toward him,
We wake him.

110

We start eating,
I see Chris eat five slices of pizza,
He drinks my soda,
I tell him to buy me another soda,
He buys me three sodas.

We're finished eating,
Chris leaves a big tip,
I see him lay down the green paper,
He puts more and more,
I want to go out.

We're finally outside,
A car comes to take us home,
Chris sent it here,
He gets inside the car,
He asks us to come,
We decide to walk home,
He drives away,
We sigh with relief.

The next morning he calls me,
He asks me to come over,
I say I'm busy.
    — Michael Bromley (E)

The following poem creates a picture of an intense, explosive person:

A person who is partly happy,
with a memory of her father's death
blocking the way
to total happiness.

A fire cracker in its last second
of silence.

A cheerful girl jumping
rope, turning the rope so quickly
that all you see is a blur.
    — Pamela Schwartzmann (E)

The next portrait links carefully selected details to compile a harsh picture of a cold, ungiving person. The image of "legs that ended in claws" (an image that may be literally and figuratively true) sets the tone. We learn about the aunt not only through what she says and does, but also through what she doesn't say and do:

Aunt Elsie

Once I had sat
cross-legged by your feet

studying the grooves and carved bottom
of your chair.
Legs that ended in claws.

My father's aunt
who never baked me cookies
ignored me because I asked too many questions
made me cry for asking your age.
My father's aunt
who always bought me slips
(the wrong size)
for every birthday and Christmas.

You were the house in Fairhaven
and the dark-walnut chair.

They took you away.
Sold your house
and gave your chair to a stranger
who smiled.

On Christmas
I did not visit you
in the cold white room
with metal chairs
where they said you lived

and when you died
I did not cry.
There is no mourning in death
the second time.
— Nanci Siller (HS)

Using behavior and attitude patterns and imagery, write someone's portrait. (The usual options apply: it can be a real person, a made-up person, or a combination.)

Persona Poem
Write a poem in the first person from the point of view of another person, real or made-up. It can be someone who appeals to you, intrigues you, or repulses you.

•

Vignette Portraits of Famous People
Books by and about famous people make readers privy to situations we don't otherwise have access to. Donald Barthelme's story "Robert Kennedy Saved From Drowning" uses vignettes and quotations to create a compelling portrait of Kennedy. The sections are titled "K. at His Desk," "Described by Secretaries," "Attitude Toward His Work," "Dress," "Gallery-

going," "K. Puzzled by His Children," "A Dream," "K. Saved From Drowning," etc. The scenes are presented so convincingly that many readers have taken them to be true; Barthelme has revealed that only "Gallery-going" is based on a real event (Barthelme happened to be there).

Take a well-known person — contemporary or historical — and write a Vignette Portrait, dealing with the private and public sides of the person from various vantage points, such as: what the person says, what others say about him or her, how the person acts in various contexts (with employees, family, strangers, media), how he or she dresses, what he or she dreams, etc. Shine the spotlight on telling moments. Merge what you know objectively about the person with what you sense intuitively. The person belongs to you while you are writing about him or her. Use techniques from the Physical and Behavioral Portrait assignments to make the character full-dimensional.

President Carter

President Carter is at the grocery store with wall to wall people around him. Trying to get out, moveless, not knowing what to do. One person says, "Don't ruin his beautiful suit, or most important his shiny shoes." So finally the owner of the store pushes everyone away and President Carter is free to go.

•

President Carter is at his hometown and everyone treats him like anyone else. Everyone is glad he is the President now. He just wants to rest and read his newspaper. He has on slippers, a white short sleeve shirt, summer pants, and a gold belt. He decided to walk down the street and say hello to his old friends. Now if President Carter walks around his friends just say, "It's nice to have you in town!" But his best friend calls him "Short Stuff." I don't think he minds what he calls him, but if everybody else does I think he would get mad.

•

President Carter is invited to a luxury restaurant and when he is going to sit down other people stand to salute him. When he sits down they give him champagne. The waiter says it's from a man across the room that thinks you are doing a great job and paid for your champagne. President Carter gets up to thank the man and asks him to join him and his family at their dinner table.

•

President Carter is at the White House. He is mad because he doesn't know what to say for a speech at a very special meeting. His daughter asks him to help her project for school and he says, "NOT NOW, YOU CAN DO IT YOURSELF!" So her mother helps her and calms President Carter down. He says "sorry" and everything's back to normal.

•

113

President Carter is in the Big City, New York. Everyone's glad to see him. He is going down the street shaking everyone's hand. They tell him their problems and he tries to help them. He cannot help all of them, but he will try hard to make them happy. President Carter is a person, too! He doesn't like being screamed at or people to complain a lot. When he comes home he sits down angrily and once more his wife calms him down.

•

President Carter is at a party. Everyone is offering him a drink, and he is covered with people. On the other side of the room there are people that don't like Carter, and they try not to look at him. All around him there are people that like him and people that don't. But he tells his friends he will not pay attention to the others. All people don't have to like him.

— Lisa Bracero (E)

Fictitious Meetings

E.L. Doctorow's novel *Ragtime* includes a scene in which Henry Ford meets J.P. Morgan. When Doctorow was asked if those two characters had indeed met, he replied that now they have. A similar device was used in Steve Allen's PBS series "Meetings of the Minds," in which historical figures from different periods sat around and chatted with each other.

Pick two or more people from literature, history, and/or who are currently famous, and bring them together, either as characters in a short story or shooting the breeze over coffee. Use the same techniques as in the previous assignment.

This assignment can be linked with books and eras the students are studying.

•

After writing about a childhood friend, a student in one of my adult workshops said, "It's almost like being with him." In one way it's better: he is different now; the person she wants to spend time with is the one from long ago. We can also write about people to get to know them better (our versions of them, that is) or to be with them before we even met them.

Two recent novels deal with the creative process by which writers re-invent people. In William Maxwell's *So Long, See You Tomorrow,* the pro-tagonist recalls a murder committed long ago by the father of a childhood friend, with whom he never came to terms. Blending memory, history (from local newspapers) and fantasy, the protagonist relives the time period, partly from the vantage point of his friend. The protagonist of Reynolds Price's *Love and Work* is an author who, working from a kernel of factual informa-tion, writes a story about how his parents, now deceased, met and courted.

Write about someone the way he or she used to be, using real and/or invented details. You can ask an old friend to reminisce about your early

114

days together, or discuss your childhoold with your parents. Or, ask your parents about their life before you were born.

•

The Party, Revisited

This is a follow-up on The Party assignment (Chapter 5), using either the same characters or creating a new cast to choose from.

It's the same party, five hours later. It turns out that they're not such a bad lot after all; under their chic exteriors and party faces are people with problems and insecurities like everyone else. Just a few guests remain; their defenses are down, and they are revealing more facets of themselves. Write a monologue of what one of the characters would say in the waning moments of the party. Or, have two or more of the characters speaking to each other.

The following poem by Cynthia McDonald includes revelations of insecurity by an amazing circus performer. Note the use of specifics to illustrate her incredible exploits and her self-punishment (which she inflicts because her self-expectations are even more extraordinary than her talent):

Breaking Seals

Even when I was only six I became aware of the talent
I had for working with seals. I trained them
To come to me when I whistled. They nuzzled their noses
Through the iron railing surrounding their pond
At the Central Park Zoo and nibbled my braids.

Now I am Esmeralda, the Seal Lady Wizard, star
Of the Circus Maroni. My seals tightrope walk,
Ride elephants, sell popcorn. They are truly astounding.
I am known here and there as the greatest seal trainer.

But I despair and must punish myself. I rend
Cascades of tissue paper till it covers the floor and
My bed, rustling me awake night after night.
I oversalt my soup and permit myself few sips of water,
Condemning myself to interior oceans. I spend months
Carving sculptures of soap which I place in the toilet.
These torments I earn by my pretense,
The pretense of being an expert seal trainer.

Lovely, slippery emblems of my skill: I know my own
Ineptitude with you, no matter what the world thinks.
I will never get you to sing the sextet from "Lucia,"
To recite the Ten Commandments, to keep your elbows
Off the table. I cannot admit that I do not know all
That there is to know about you. I can only confide
My ignorance to you because seals do not have ears.

32
Concept Personification

By invoking the "personification clause" in their poetic licenses, writers can make rocks talk or trees sit down to dinner. Another application of personification is to embody a concept in human form. "Everyman" and other Morality plays feature such characters as Good Fellowship, Good Sense, Lust, and Death.

"Death" has gone on to make many movie and literary appearances, usually in the guise of the Grim Reaper. In Ingmar Bergman's film "The Seventh Seal," a doomed man challenges Death to a chess game, a scene parodied in the short film called "The Dove," in which the game is badminton. Woody Allen romps off to the Beyond in a dance with Death at the end of "Love and Death," and he writes about a visit from Death in his playlet "Death Knocks," in which a weary, clumsy Death comes to claim a dress manufacturer; this time the game is gin rummy. The dress manufacturer wins and decides at the end that Death is a "schlep."

Other concept personifications are Father Time, Uncle Sam, Cupid, and Opportunity (about whom we know little, except for the tendency to knock rather than use the bell). Possibilities for new ones include: Wisdom, Stupidity, Insanity, or Magic.

Personify any concept and use the embodiment in a poem or story. You can write in the voice of the personification ("I am Mr. Love, and if I don't get the divorce rate down my job is in trouble,") or from the point of view of someone encountering the figure. Other possibilities are to write a third person story or a skit (like Woody Allen's "Death Knocks"); have two or more personifications get together to compare notes; or directly address the personification.

Mr. Magic

Do you believe in magic?
Well, let me tell you
I'm the spark
Of all Abbra Caddabra
Everywhere
Over here, over there
Have you heard of the Magical Mystery Tour?
Well, I don't want to brag, but
I was the tour guide
Heard of Melvin?
I gave him his start
In a rundown castle cafe
Heard of black top hats and rabbits?
Touché my friend
That's me
Of course you can't see me

It's all in the wrists
You know
                    — Tony Pena (HS)

33
Interior Monologues

Through the interior monologue — presentation of a character's unspoken thoughts — fiction writers enable readers to read minds. Describe a fictional situation to the class, and ask students to write an applicable interior monologue (in prose or poetry). For example: *Doris is on her way home to the farm after her freshman year at a big-city college. She has changed; she has had more "worldly" experiences in a year than her parents have had in a lifetime. She is going to be spending time with her family and old friends and is wondering whether she'll be able to communicate with them. She is also thinking about the things about home that she has missed. Write an interior monologue for Doris.*

•

Students can write interior monologues for literary or historical figures, such as Captain Ahab, alone on the deck in the middle of the night, musing about Moby (or, Moby musing about the Captain); Dr. Jeckyl as he is turning into Mr. Hyde; Columbus, on a moonless night, deep into his voyage; or Holden Caulfield wondering about other things like where the Central Park ducks go for the winter.

Another way to approach this is for students to write the poems these people might write. Or, you can ask the students to write their own versions of actual interior monologues, such as the "To be or not to be" soliloquy; what would Hamlet think at that juncture if the student, rather than Shakespeare, supplied Hamlet's brain with thoughts?

34
Someone New in the House

Little brothers and sisters often show up in students' writings, portrayed as brats whose function is to get their older siblings in trouble.

Here are some other aspects to focus on:

The moment when you discover that a baby brother or sister is on the way. How was it told to you, or did you find out by eavesdropping? What was your reaction?

The changes in the household as the pregnancy developed.

The time of birth getting near. Your mother going to the hospital.

The first visual images of the baby at the hospital and at home; images of people interacting with the child.

Coming to terms—jealousies, new tasks ("You're going to have more responsibility around here"), and the evolving relationship between you and the child.

How it is now—but tell us about more than punches and trouble; give the kid a break and also tell us what good things he or she has added to your life.

These and other moments of heightened experience with little brothers and sisters can be used as starting points for writing. Students should avoid writing *about* the situation, but rather unfold it before the reader's eyes, with nuances and shadings. Instead of saying, "Having a baby brother can take attention away from you," students should dramatize that phenomenon perhaps by presenting a scene in which the older sibling is ignored, so that the reader will draw the same conclusion.

Although only those with younger brothers and sisters can write from direct experience, others can write a fantasy about having a younger sibling; write about younger cousins; or, if they have older siblings, project themselves into an older brother or sister's place. An alternative is to write about being an only child.

We wait so long, the phone doesn't ring.
It's 5:00 or maybe 6:00 when we hear the news —
It's a boy, I have a brother.
I really don't care, I want to go home.
Two weeks later, I hold him in my arms,
the mass of dark, fuzzy hair gently brushing across my arm.
He cries.
Four weeks later I give him a bottle, I watch the anxious
    little mouth grab the nipple desperately.
He doesn't want any more.
One year later he gives me a bear-hug.
It's time for a nap.
I think I love him, I don't know.
Six years later we talk, he needs my help.
I love him now — he calls my name.
        He loves me, too.
                        — Geri Lee (HS)

My Mother Having My Sister

My mother was having a baby. She was getting fatter and fatter. It was the night of March 24th, 1971. I slept with my mother, thinking that this would keep my mother from going to the hospital. In the middle of the night I woke up with an earache. My neighbor was there and told me my parents were at the hospital. After a couple of hours my father came and brought me the medicine for my earache. He then left. I fell asleep after that. When I woke up, my father was there telling me to get dressed and we'll go visit my mother. My neighbor gave me a bouquet of flowers to give to my mother. I thought my mother would be dancing around the room, but when we got there I saw her all white and weak lying in bed. My sister, all pink and happy, was next to her, kicking her legs while she slept.

                        — Anna Pollatos (E)

120

35
Who Would March in Your Parade

Visualize looking out your window and seeing a parade go by. But instead of St. Patrick's Day or Memorial Day, it is "Your Day." People, objects, places, foods, and words that are meaningful to you march by. Write what you see marching in your parade. Be specific. If including your "favorite blue jeans," describe the holes in the knees and pockets, the texture, etc. Don't merely say, "My friend Bobby from summer camp," but describe the expression on Bobby's face and perhaps a placard he is carrying. Places can march by, or even ideas (a group of words that you like). Dig deeply into your past. Describe the floats. What is the band playing?

A sense of the writer's character should emerge from the items in the parade. This assignment can be fun, and it provides practice in writing short, visual descriptions. Students are likely to include material that can be used in future writings; perhaps a long-forgotten friend will march by, or an incident from the past will be acted out.

Bing-Bong Dropalong Parade

Wow! How neat! Look, there's my favorite dessert coming. Chocolate pudding with whipped cream and a cherry on top. This is great. Oh! And here comes a big bunch of purple lilacs that I picked up in California last year. How beautiful they look. Oh, and here comes my old friend Kate! Oh how nice she looks. Her brown hair got longer and for the first time in so many years she is wearing that red shirt I gave her! Oh, look. Here comes mashed potatoes with steak! Oh, I'm getting hungry. And here comes my pink sweater which I have worn for a year, washing and wearing, washing and wearing! This sure brings back memories! And look, here comes my bunny rabbit. Oh! His ears look longer, his nose is bright red, his blue eyes how they shine, and his pink and white fur, how clean and shiny it looks. Look! Here comes my *Cat in the Hat* book which I've read so many times. But now it looks a little dirty because I spilled some orange juice on it.

Look! Here comes my good ol' buddy Connie! Oh, how nice she looks! Her long dark brown hair glitters and her long eyelashes, wow! And look at her beautiful yellow dress. And she even lost weight! Look! Here comes the Christmas tree! The one I decorated all by myself! But the only thing I put on it was the big yellow star. Look, you can see it right there. And a few red balls, all the same color. It may not be good looking but it sure means something special to me.

And look! Here come the juicy oranges I ate back in California, and the very first cake I baked back in Gramma's little house. The cake does look good if I say so myself and it tastes good too. Its strawberry frosting with banana filling tasted so good. Oh no, here comes my math paper! This must mean the parade is finishing! Oh no, how sad!

—Monica Dibono (E)

36
Letters That Can't
Be Delivered

For most people, the receipt of an important personal letter is more anxiously anticipated than the latest bestseller. The bestseller is generally read and discarded, while the letter is reread and carefully put away. Non-writers are also more likely to have a meaningful experience with language in writing a letter than they are in writing, say, a few lines of verse.

Many authors use letter writing to explore ideas and images, or as a cure for writer's block. Letters take away some of the ambiguity from writing by providing an audience of one. Once you have filled in the word following "Dear," the rest often comes naturally.

The following assignments involve letters that can't be delivered, so they require a suspension of disbelief. Students should select "recipients" they have feelings about, be they feelings of attraction, repulsion, or curiosity. This is their chance to communicate with the unreachable, asking any questions they want. The optional next step for these assignments is to have students write replies to their own letters, or to pass the letters around for others to answer.

I've sometimes asked very young students to imagine that they have a "magic stamp," which can send letters to people who have died, or to objects. Many children love to draw their version of the stamp.

Letters to Objects
People often have strong feelings toward the objects around them. Sometimes we express these feelings through action — giving the reluctant car a kick in the rear bumper — but much is left unsaid lest one get caught having a conversation with a fork.

Letters to objects provide a connection between the writer and his or her environment. The possibilities are as varied as the objects in the universe. The reply letters often contain "human" statements such as the window who writes, "The only time I move is when someone breaks me," or the car who complains, "What bothers me is when people push on my pedals and make me go faster. Then before you know it they're pressing me to stop."

Solicit suggestions for possible objects to be written to, and list them on the board. Students have written to a pen, sneakers, blackboard, car, bed, desk, yoyo, window, mirror, candy bar, garbage can, numbers, eyeglasses, lamppost, paper, and sidewalk.

Dear Blackboard,

I can't stand you. Everyday I come to school and I have to wash all the chalk dust off you. You repay me by having homework assignments waiting for me. Don't you care about anybody? Do you know how much ink I waste every night I go home? You have no consideration for anybody. But you know what, you must be very lonely watching all the kids pass you by year after year. So I apologize for all the things I said.

Your friend,
Reuben

Dear Reuben,

I'm sorry I show you no consideration. I'm sorry I give you homework and make you waste ink. You see it's my only way to communicate with you. If there was any other way with you I would use it. I'm very lonely. Do you know how it feels to just sit and watch people grow into maturity and you can't participate? It's happening now. Just think how you were in 7th grade. You were just a child. For three years I watched you grow into a man. All that time I wanted to lead you and guide you the right way. The only way was to give you homework. I hope you will forgive me. See you in school.

Write soon,
Blackboard

P.S. Don't use so much water tomorrow, because it gives me the snuffles.

— Reuben Jenkins (M)

Letters to Nature

This is an offshoot of Letters to Objects. Past recipients have included animals, insects, plants, flowers, stars, planets, and volcanoes.

Dear Tobacco,

O tobacco, you destroyed my mother
You ruined her life, & now she's gone
She'll never be back, all because of you
You drove her into smoking you
but not of her own free will

124

I want you destroyed
stop bringing death to all.
                    — Michele

Dear Michele,
It's not my fault believe me.
Man has made me into a cigarette.
I'd like to grow free
but man takes over me.
I hate death and want to eliminate it.
They saw me off & add chemicals too
They set me on fire & let me burn
Do you think I like being smoked?
                    — Michele Ondey (M)

Letters to Parts of the Body
Students have written to their hair, freckles, fingernails, etc.

Dear Hair,
I think you should be curly.
But my mother thinks you're beautiful
when you're clean.
I don't like combing you
and washing you.
It's nice to have you blowing in
the wind all clean and fresh.
But why don't you just become brushed
when you're knotted
like a horse's freshly brushed hair
blowing in the wind
as it rides fast and flashing.
I love you sometimes hair.
                    Love, Jenny

Dear Jenny,
I'm sorry I'm not curly
but long straight and dark is pretty too.
I need taking care of because
I will be blowing fresh and clean
like a waterfall.
                    Love, Hair
                    — Jenny Klein (E)

Letters to People Who Died
The medium of writing allows us to imagine doing what the other kind of medium claims to be able to arrange: a "visit" with people who have died. When people die, we realize that there were things we never got to say

125

to them, including our feelings about their death. Some people continue to live inside us and are incorporated into our inner voices. "Speaking" to the dead — be it through seances or poetry — may really be an attempt to reach part of ourselves.

Many students find that writing a letter-poem to someone who died has therapeutic value. Due to the sensitive nature of the subject matter, give students the option of making up someone to write to, or writing to someone they didn't know, or writing another kind of letter.

In order to engage the reader, students should convey a sense of who the person was, using physical details and other techniques discussed in the People unit (chapter 31).

To My Sister,
I wish you hadn't died when you were born. Now all I have is two brothers. Sometimes I think I like sisters better than brothers. My mother tells me if you had lived I might not have been born or we would have 4 children. If we had 4 children I would probably have to share a room with you. Sometimes I would mind but sometimes I wouldn't. My brothers say they are glad you did not live. My mother says your name would have been Jennifer and we'd call you Jenny. You had blondish brownish hair. You would be about 19 or 20 now. I have brown hair past my shoulders. It's too bad you died. I wish you could have lived.

Love,
Katey

To Katey,
For the one minute that I was alive, I saw our mother with a pale look on her face. The doctors and nurses just shook their heads. All of a sudden everything went blank. It must be fun to be alive. That's all I can say for the minute I was alive.

From your sister,
Jenny
— Katey Bernard (E)

Grandpa,
I see you standing there,
with your brown suit and polka dot tie,
the gray hairs neatly combed,
then sitting solemnly like a chauffeur
as you drive us to your house
from the airport,
or sitting serenely in your easy chair,
with the newspaper hiding your face.
Grandpa,
I see us standing there
playing poke-in-the-nose,
I see your smile while we open
our Christmas presents.

Grandpa,
why'd you die?

You never yelled,
but let us know in a quiet way,
just a look, not mean, but stern
    that was all.
When we would visit
you would seem happy,
not the laughing kind,
but the happiness of love.
You tried not to let on,
but it was obvious,
in your manner, in your soft blue eyes,
underneath that stern mask, you
    were really a softie.
Grandpa, why'd you die?
          — Abi Caplovitz (E)

Letters to Figures from History or Literature

History
      Students write to an historical figure, asking questions and telling the recipient how the world has changed in the intervening years. The reply letters should answer those questions and describe what life was like in the past. (This is a refreshing approach to writing a history paper.)

Literature
      Students write to a character from a novel or story. A good work of fiction makes its characters come alive; when you finish a novel it is almost like a friend has moved, never to be heard from again (unless the author writes a sequel). This is a way of keeping in touch with those characters.

Hate Mail
      Perhaps this should go under the heading "Letters That *Shouldn't* Be Delivered." *Write a nasty letter; it could be to a store manager who is abusive to kids, a politician you disagree with, or anyone who has wronged you. Often there is no person responsible for unpleasantries, but you can make up such a person; for example, you could write to the inventor of rejection. Or, you could write to a real person unknown to you, such as the inventor of the wrapping for packaged cheese that is impossible to open without demolishing it with a knife.*

Dear Rich Uncle Charlie,
      Now that you are dead I hate your guts. When you were alive I liked you very much. (I liked your wallet even more). I can remember when I came to your mansion. We would make paper boats with 50 dollar bills. Then we

would send them away in your river. You let me make airplanes with savings bonds and traveler's checks and send them out the window. You had a great bathtub. I always went scuba diving in it. To get me to do my homework you would say "Time is money" and flash a roll of twenties in my face. On holidays you would fly me in your private Boeing 747 to Las Vegas, Miami, Hollywood, and Texas. I made friends with your 36,297,451,082 maids and butlers. The reason I am sore at you is all you left me was your 59¢ pen and one of your goldfish.

— Alex Omura (E)

37
Creation

James Tate's poem "Teaching the Ape to Write Poems" begins "They didn't have much trouble / teaching the ape to write poems" and ends with the words which, when whispered into the ape's ear, get him started on his literary career. No, they don't bribe the ape with bananas. That might work until the ape is full, but Tate offers a more sustained inspiration.

Read the poem to the class, stopping before the last two lines; ask if anyone can guess the teaching secret. There have been some interesting suggestions, but no one has come up with Tate's conclusion:

Teaching the Ape to Write Poems

They didn't have much trouble
teaching the ape to write poems:
first they strapped him into the chair,
then tied the pencil around his hand
(the paper had already been nailed down).
Then Dr. Bluespire leaned over his shoulder
and whispered into his ear:
"You look like a god sitting there.
Why don't you try writing something?"

Flattery will get you everywhere. Anyone sitting over a blank paper with a pen or pencil (or, as songwriter Phil Ochs once said, "I sat, pen in hand, over my typewriter") is a god for that unformed world below (although it's doubtful that anyone has surpassed that great first line, "Let there be light.") Vicente Huidobro ends his poem "Ars Poetica" with a touch of humility: "The poet is a *little* God" (emphasis mine).

This assignment is an exercise in ex-cathedra writing. Discuss Tate's poem and the opening of Genesis, and ask students to bring light and life to their paper by creating a "world" (or part of one) on the page, perhaps starting with "Let there be. . . ." Once a world is established on the paper, the students can continue to play god by manipulating their creations.

Not all students are nice gods. One student ended his piece with "They turn it into a tourist attraction" and turned over his paper, but a couple of minutes later he added, "Then it rained for three years and wiped out everything." He smiled impishly and said, "That's not nice, but I did it." He was aware of the power of writing, a power that can be used beneficently or cruelly.

The thrust of this assignment applies to all writing: to make something out of nothing; to experience the pen or pencil as a tool in your service rather than as an unbudging foreign object; to perceive the blank paper as possibility, not intimidation. This is getting to sound like a sermon, but all writers need a little, uh, faith.

Parents of the World

Let there be a child playing on the stairs. She should be happy and joyous with nothing to worry about. Another child should come along and play with her. Let them go out into the open world and get acquainted. Let them grow together and experience everything. Let them get an education and get a job. Let them get married and produce a family of their own. Let them be parents of the world!

—Isabel Feliz (E)

38
Fantasy

The ability to fantasize is an asset not only in the arts but also in math, science, or any other discipline. Einstein said, "When I examine myself and my methods of thought, I come to the conclusion that the gift of fantasy has meant more to me than my talent for absorbing positive knowledge." Fantasy helps people pass the time; cope with unpleasant, boring, hostile, and difficult situations; work out problems; order the future; and relive or reorder the past. Sometimes I get myself to start or keep writing by fantasizing that I'm a great writer, much in demand.

There are parts of ourselves we don't act out. The loyal bank teller dreams of larceny; the office worker fantasizes pouring coffee on the boss's new suit; the child spies on his or her own funeral, gloating over how miserable everyone is; the dieter consumes with the "mind's stomach" several banana splits followed by dessert; the Supreme Court Justice, tired of casting a sober shadow, shows up in Times Square wearing a tutu and sombrero. Any fantasy can be incorporated into a satisfying writing experience.

In school there are fantasies going on at any given moment, even during the most interesting classes. Fantasies *about* school abound. In Maureen Strange's novel *Beginners,* the protagonist, Bessie, doesn't feel like she fits in at her suburban high school. Her misery is mitigated by making a new friend and discovering fantasy:

> ...she wasn't alone! He [her new friend] was her moral support, her protection against the armies of polyannas and jocks and cheerleaders and clubbies who cluttered her daily life with their costumes and routines and pantomimes and antics like some dizzying Technicolor freak show. And with this new moral support she soon developed, in a skewed sort of way, a sense of humor....For one thing, she learned to fantasize.

At school, she passed the time imagining what would happen if, say, every fraternity and sorority sweater in the whole place suddenly disappeared. The members of Beta Xhi and Delta Rho would be milling around in the halls not knowing who to say hi to or give the club sign to. . . . In a few hours the sweaters would be returned but somehow a few of them would be given by mistake to various unneat people, leaving the ones who'd been deprived of their sweaters to run around the halls trying to prove their identity ("Wait! You don't understand! I'm — *Wait!* Come back!"). . . .

In her fantasy, Bessie alters the pecking order by casting a spell on club sweaters, the scorecards by which the in-people can tell the players from the non-players. Who has not fantasized achieving a new position in the pecking order, or pecking away at that order until it is in shambles?

But Bessie's favorite fantasy is one in which she shoos away the whole shebang. During the homeroom period PA announcements, she fantasizes that a mysterious voice interrupts the class secretary's invitation to tryouts for "Paint Your Wagon" by saying:

> We interrupt this broadcast to bring you the following bulletin: Due to circumstances beyond anyone's control, and for reasons no one particularly cares to explain at this time, High School has been canceled. Although this is indeed cause for alarm for most of you crummy little bastards out there, we must ask you to please not panic, but simply follow your homeroom teacher's instructions for the standard fire drill, just as you've been following them year in and year out for the length of your pathetic and fun-filled career as a ward of the Board of Education, and form a double line in the corridor and head quickly and quietly, so as not to disturb the seriousness of the occasion, for the nearest emergency exit.
>
> Do not stop along the way to gather mementos; looseleafs which have been autographed by your fellow wretches, and Varsity jock straps and G.O. cards and the like, because you will not need them where you are going. Not only will they fail to get you a single penny in trade at the local hock shop, but they undoubtedly will cause you untold distress and humiliation should you attempt to show them to strangers on the street who, after regarding the items with a lack of appreciation that is total, will probably burst into gales of laughter so intense as to knock you right off balance and onto the ground, doing irreparable damage to your cool, not to mention sending your proud momentos into a nearby puddle in the gutter where they will be hopelessly water-damaged and rendered useless to you in your decrepit old age as a wistful reminder of what a hotshot you were in your prime.
>
> Therefore dally not on your way to the emergency exit, where you will be greeted by an unpleasant-faced individual who will grin sardonically as he asks you to please remove your class ring and drop it into the bubbling cauldron to your right where it will be melted down and eventually become part of the ornate and gaudy decoration on the facade of the Tomb of the Unknown Booster, which has been donated anonymously and is now under construction out on the baseball diamond, as no doubt one or two of you more alert bozos have already noticed, when last you slid into third and

rammed into a pile of bricks. . . We wish you luck in your life-long pursuit of a reason for being and an underling to dump on, and now, please rise for a final singing of "The Star-Spangled Banner."

Write a school fantasy, such as Bessie's about the disappearance of the sweaters.

Write a fantasy of what you might say if you seized control of the PA system and had the attention of the entire school.

Write any other fantasy — within the bounds of appropriate taste for your classroom — that you might have had recently or are having right now as I am describing this assignment.

•

The Person within the Person

Another way of approaching fantasy is for students to think of the "person within the person." Students could write about a Jeckyl/Hyde situation, or one in which an individual expresses positive hidden aspects of the self. Many young people leave their families and hometowns in an attempt to discover and express that "person within the person." Some people are required to relegate parts of their personality to the realm of fantasy because of their social position, such as a minister, teacher, or politician.

Write in the persona of a character whose exterior personality differs from his or her interior sense of self. Don't just tell about the differences, but dramatize them with events and fantasies.

Fantasy vs. Reality

Fantasy is rarely duplicated by reality. We anticipate an event, "preliving" it in our minds, yet it hardly ever turns out the way we envisioned it. In most cases, reality comes up short, but there are times when things actually turn out better than in our "wildest dreams."

Such wish-fulfillment fantasies as "dancing on Broadway" or "running in the Olympics" can help close the gap between fantasy and reality: "I always had this dream that one day I'd be a great musician, so I worked and worked at it, and now here I am in the Philharmonic."

Discuss how students' previous fantasies about forthcoming events have compared with the actual events. Also, what might happen if a wish-fulfillment fantasy, such as being a rock star, were to come true; what would it *really* be like?

Write about fantasy/reality; here are two approaches:

1) Write about a fantasy that actually came true, first writing the fantasy and then the actual experience. For example, if you moved from one town to another, you could write your fantasy of the new location, followed by what it was really like.

133

Gosh! Am I curious. I can't wait to get out. I think I'm going to give this place a kick. "Boom!" God told me what I was going to be when I got out: a "Cuff." When I get out there's gonna be yellow rocks with blue fingers on them. Then I'll be baptized in a running waterfall. Then I'll look around and I'll see orange mountains with totally green trees and purple peaks. I'll register with a tribe and be a beautiful prince with a brown crown and a white leaf around my private parts. And. . . .

Hold up. I'm being pulled. Pop. I'm out in the world. Uck. A white room with green guys leaning over me and chanting, "It's a boy, Ms. Cuff, it's a boy." Oh my god, this guy hitting me. Ouch. "Hey, God, I want out."

— David Cuff (E)

New York!

I used to live in California and when I heard we were moving to New York I was scared. I mean I thought it was going to be rreeeaally rough. I actually thought King Kong lived on the Empire State Building and whenever anyone walked down on the street below him he would step on them. I thought gangsters roamed the streets that were so mean that the police were afraid of them! I thought that the only thing the kids care about are video games. I thought everywhere you went there were crazies screaming their heads off about the end of the world, and you couldn't walk 8 blocks without being mugged!

But I was wrong. Actually I got to like it! There was a lot of hustle and bustle that makes the city come to life. There aren't that many kooks and I haven't been mugged yet! My favorite part of the city is downtown, around Times Square. There are a lot of pretzel and chestnut vendors and I love their smell. I see some gangs now and then but I don't say anything to them and they don't do anything to me.

In California I never saw snow and when I did for the first time I began to think the crazies were right about the end of the world!

It's rough at times but if it wasn't then it would be boring. And in the 7 years I've been here I've never seen King Kong!

— Luke Ratray (E)

2) Write a grand, wish-fulfillment fantasy and then write about what you think would happen if it really came true: a fantasy about a fantasy coming true. The key is to inject reality into the second fantasy. For example, a fantasy about being an Olympic gold medalist might be full of praise, crowds, and adulation for your soaring majestic beauty on the gymnastics mat. But the "reality fantasy" might also include hard work, frustration, sweat, pain, demanding coaches, annoying journalists, doubts about your ability, missing the opportunity to play with friends, and a lack of privacy.

The material gathered from these assignments might contain the makings of a story. Students often write wish-fulfillment stories that are one-dimensional and unconvincing. These can be fun, but stories that fuse fantasy and reality tend to make for better reading.

39
Dream Objects

Charles Simic's poem "Dream-Tree" tells of a tree that takes root in a fertile imagination and flowers on the page. Simic's imagery conveys the tree's enormousness and magical qualities. Slowly read the poem out loud in a darkened room and let the tree grow in the minds of the students.

Dream-Tree

I have dreamed of a strange tree
Where poppies and apples grow together.
When the dew falls from its leaves
They turn to precious stones.
In my backyard they bring the light of Easter Sundays
All throughout the summer night.

High the preying chickenhawk soars,
Still higher the tree climbs.
It spreads across the state of Indiana.
The leaves fall around Gary.
The scent drifts across Michigan and Ohio.

Write about your own Dream-Object. Some possibilities: Dream-House, Dream-Pet, Dream-Meal, Dream-School, Dream-Flower, Dream-Car, Dream-Toy. Or, you could write about Dream-People, such as a Dream-Parent, Dream-Teacher, Dream-Friend, or Dream-Team.

40
Interviews

> Interview? Oh, dear.... Well, yes, I suppose so... but not a list of questions or a third degree, I hope.... I was interviewed a short time ago.... Terrible.... Couldn't we just talk together?....
> —Isak Dineson, from the beginning of her *Paris Review* interview

There is a difference between questioning and interviewing. Many student interviewers make a list of questions and ask them in order. These "questioners" go from Question #3 to #4, even if #4 has been dealt with in the answer to #2, or #3 hasn't been answered fully, or the answer to #3 contained a revelation begging for a question not on the list.

An interview should be a guided conversation, with the interviewer occasionally checking the question list to make sure important areas aren't being ignored. During the best interviews, one hardly refers to the list, and discovers at the end that everything has been covered, and more. A skilled interviewer can inspire the subject to say something for the first time — to arrive at an insight or make a connection not previously articulated — or to say something he or she did not plan to reveal.

Interview someone; it could be a politician, local celebrity, or anyone else with interesting things to say. Prepare for the interview with whatever research is feasible, such as reading what has been written about the person, talking to people who know him or her, or learning about the person's area of expertise.

Write up the interview in narrative form, describing the person, the setting, and any revealing facial expressions and gestures. If possible, tape-record the interview, so you won't have to worry about quoting accurately. If you can, spend some time with the subject at work and/or home.

41
Headlines

The most concentrated, disciplined writing I've ever done under pressure was to compose headlines for my college newspaper. Headlines have to grab and inform the reader in a few words. I did a lot of rewriting.

Cut out some articles from a newspaper, snip off the headlines, and ask students to write their own headlines. Then bring headline writing into everyday life.

Imagine yourself as a headline writer for incidents that would not be reported by newspapers, such as an argument between a brother and a sister: "Brat Brother Strikes Again." Like many newspapers, amplify the main headline with second and third tiers:

BRAT BROTHER STRIKES AGAIN
Rampage Disrupts Sister's Piano Lesson
Recriminations Promised

Next, title the incident as if it were a movie, and add "grabber" lines for the advertisements:

"ATTACK OF THE BRAT"
He came from nowhere...
His mind is nowhere...
...But the sister got her revenge!

42
Ghostwriting

The demand for books by actors, politicians, and athletes has made ghostwriting into a growing source of work for writers. Lately, the ghostwriter has been getting cover credit more frequently ("By Lassie, as barked to Sam Typewriter"). There is another kind of ghostwriting, for which authors hardly ever get credit: speechwriting.

When Presidents, Senators, social activists, and others in the Public Ear give speeches, it's likely that some or all of what they say originated in the typewriter of a salaried wordsmith. Spiro Agnew's notorious epithet against the media, "nattering nabobs of negativity," was composed by William Safire, then a White House speechwriter. What would happen if all people were called upon to write memoirs or issue speeches at various junctures in their lives—and had ghostwriters working for them?

Ghost a memoir or speech for either a typical client (politician) or an unlikely one (a derelict). You can write realistically or satirically. Here are some premises:

MEMOIRS: Write an excerpt from anyone's memoir—a celebrity or a "common" person, real or imagined. You can make this an extended project by actually collaborating with someone on his or her memoirs, perhaps an elderly neighbor or a local shopkeeper.

RESIGNATION SPEECHES: Write a resignation speech for a government official who has been wracked with scandal (he or she can be innocent or guilty); a teacher who is fed up with his or her class; or anyone who feels unappreciated.

ACCEPTANCE SPEECHES: Write an acceptance speech for someone winning a major award, such as an Oscar ("I'd like to thank my dog and my eighth grade science teacher, who---"), or a fictitious award (Best Crossing Guard, Top Parent).

INAUGURAL ADDRESS: Write an inaugural address for the next President, or for anyone assuming any office or position (King of the Hobos).

CONFESSION: Write a police station or courtroom confession for a criminal, including the events leading up to the crime, and, perhaps, mitigating circumstances. Or, write a confession for anyone accused of wrongdoing in his or her personal life.

43
Everything but the Book

This extension of the Titles assignment (chapter 14) encompasses everything that goes into a hardcover edition. . .except the book itself: title; author's name; publisher's comments (including plot summary and praise for the book and/or author); blurbs (endorsements by well-known people); author's biography; and, if you make this a writing/art project, cover design and author's photo. For nonfiction books, students could also include a table of contents and index.

In preparation, students should spend a half hour or so in a bookstore or library scrutinizing the way books are packaged. This assignment lends itself to parody, although it is hard to distinguish the real thing from parody when some books are adorned with jacket copy such as this, for *The Running Man:*

> THE PERFECT CRIME calls for the perfect criminal—and Rex Buchanan had all the equipment. He was a big, good-looking man with stainless steel nerves and a hair trigger brain.
>
> Rex had the perfect partner, a lovely, gifted, bright-eyed girl named Paula. She was so utterly in love with Rex there was nothing she wouldn't do for him.
>
> And so it began. And soon they found that one perfect crime leads to another—and another. . .

Denim and Silk by Rhea Kelasey is billed by its publisher as having symbolism that is "vivid and unique, used in the common theme of a relationship destroying itself. It is a story told with humor and honesty, malice and irony. It is a book of philosophy which tells us much about ourselves and the human consciousness." Under a photo of the author is the following copy:

Rhea Kelasey is the author of the much praised *Chalk,* which is about a group of young people trying to develop a perfect community in the woods. In *Denim and Silk,* her second novel, Rhea writes about two people in Mexico trying to find themselves, and, when they do, looking for someone to share "themselves" with. Later they find out that they never really knew "themselves" at all.

Rhea Kelasey is presently living in San Francisco, but has a home in Mexico that she goes to often. She paints frequently and is an active participant in art shows throughout California.

When in California, don't try to look up Rhea, and don't bother asking for *Denim and Silk* at your local bookstore. They are both the invention of high school student Lindsay Ahl.

Here are two blurbs for fictitious books:

The rosy fingers of dawn rose from this book. Zeus should kneel before her. — Homer
— Laura Fisher (HS)

I have finally met another nobody! I lift my hat off to you! — E. Dickenson
— Kathryn Lambert (HS)

As a follow-up, students can write a review of their own or someone else's "book."

•

This assignment could be combined with Invent a Poet (chapter 79) to produce Everything *Including* the Book.

A similar assignment can be done for record album covers, including liner notes, lyrics, and a biography of the singer or group.

44
Advertising

Advertising copywriters devote more attention—and get paid more—per word than most other writers. They use such literary devices as metaphor, alliteration, punning, and juxtaposition. Like poetry, ads must say a lot with a few words, in a convincing and memorable way.

Ask students to write copy for a TV, radio, poster, or newspaper advertising campaign. The advertisements can be for an imaginary product—either something to meet a real demand (room-cleaner) or something frivolous (shoe tie-er, banana peeler); an existing product; a public service campaign (solar energy); or an upcoming school event.

As preparation for writing their own copy, students should bring in ads from newspapers and magazines, and transcriptions of TV and radio commercials. Discuss the literary devices and other approaches used in these ads; how is language manipulated in order to manipulate the consumer? Distinguish between ads that dazzle or amuse the reader, and ads that present information.

You can make this into an extended unit that not only heightens students' ability to use language strategically, but also makes them more aware of how advertising attempts to affect their behavior.

The visual component of print and television advertisements is as important as the language. You can make this into a writing/art project by having students do visuals for their ads, perhaps resulting in an exhibit.

45
Treatments

Movie and television projects are often developed in "steps"; a premise may lead to a treatment to a first draft to a revised script and finally to production. Discuss the premises behind some movies and television series (a "high concept" premise—a recent addition to Hollywood jargon—can consist of only a phrase). Then ask the students to write their own premises, an exercise combining conceptualization and concision.

A *treatment* is a present tense prose synopsis of the proposed script. The emphasis is on plot and character development, with tidbits of dialogue and description. When I wrote a movie treatment I had to present scenes with broad strokes, sometimes violating the "show, don't tell" tenet by saying things such as "They continue to argue and all the hostility that has been building up comes pouring out" (a line that would be *verboten* in most short stories). Since the story in a treatment is condensed, each paragraph might result in several pages of screenplay. I constantly had to make story advancement decisions. That was taxing on the imagination, but it was a relief to be able to move so quickly through a story.

Someone writing for the camera must think visually—something must always be *happening* on the screen. A screenwriter in F. Scott Fitzgerald's story "Teamed With Genius" describes his approach as, "You just get behind the camera and dream."

Since there is usually not enough time for writing extended fiction in school workshops, an assignment in treatment writing could be an opportunity for students to think big without doing the detail work (the prospect of which can preempt effort). An ambitious student can follow up the treatment with a portion of the screenplay.

Write a treatment for a movie or a TV pilot. A TV pilot treatment should include a paragraph explaining the setting and the regular characters.

A Movie Treatment — Part One

My movie is about a boy moving from the country to the city. You see him packing up and putting everything into the car in the beginning.

You see a close-up of his face with a sad expression. Then it switches to the countryside around him: grass, mountains, trees and small animals. He is in the car as he sees how things change around him. He says, "Dad, will I find any friends in the city?" His father tells him about all the children in the city. He still feels unhappy.

After a while they come to the city. He's amazed at all of the tall buildings and bridges. He looks all around him, as you see cars, people, buildings and buses.

When they get to their own building, he asks, "Is this all ours?" His father shows him their apartment and tells him about the city.

When he is in bed, he says to himself, "I hope I like it here."

In the morning he wakes up and looks out the window expecting to see a green mountain (you see him earlier in the film looking out his window in the country and seeing a mountain). He finds a red brick building standing in front of him.

He gets his clothes on and walks through the house, looking for the kitchen. He sees a note telling him that his parents have left for a little while and that he should go exploring.

You see him eat his breakfast and walk outside.

— Michael Bromley (E)

46
New Proverbs

Every kid has heard — probably to the point of tedium — that "an apple a day keeps the doctor away," or "you can't have your cake and eat it, too." Gather some other traditional proverbs from your students and discuss how they say a lot very quickly, usually via figurative language.

Many proverbs deal on the literal level with one situation while also working metaphorically, such as the call for preventative sewing, "A stitch in time saves nine." Other proverbs work *only* as metaphor, such as "Don't cut off your nose to spite your face."

We've heard some proverbs so many times that we don't really listen to the way language conveys the messages. Read the students some proverbs they probably have not heard before, asking them to concentrate on the way the proverbs *sound* as well as on what they mean. Here are some African proverbs:

> When a man comes toward you, you need not say, "Come here."
> Cactus is bitter only to him who tastes of it.
> I have a cow in the sky but cannot drink her milk.
> Earth is the queen of beds.
> Don't try to make someone hate the person he loves, for he will go on loving, but he will hate you.

These proverbs were written by William Blake in the 1790s:

> The road to excess leads to the palace of wisdom.
> No bird soars too high, if he soars with his own wings.
> The cut worm forgives the plow.

More than a century after Blake, two young French surrealist poets — Paul

Eluard (who edited a magazine called *Proverbe)* and Benjamin Péret — collaborated on "surrealist proverbs." Here is a sampling, translated by Bill Zavatsky:

> Sleep that is singing makes the shadows tremble.
> Whoever moves disappears.
> A crab by any other name won't forget the sea.
> Elephants are contagious.
> Animals don't need stitches.
> The sun doesn't shine for anyone.
> When the road is done, do it again.
> I came, I sat down, I left.
> Dance rules over the white forest.
> You've read everything but drunk nothing.

A couple of these proverbs are take-offs on established proverbs ("A crab by any other name won't forget the sea" is a reincarnation of Shakespeare's "a rose by any other name would smell as sweet"); some use the rhythm of a proverb to house an exciting manipulation of language ("Sleep that is singing makes the shadows tremble."); while others are straightforward ("You've read everything but drunk nothing.")

Tell the class it's time for some new proverbs. Students should each write a batch of proverbs, which can be serious or silly, make sense or nonsense. This is their chance to make public the wisdom they have garnered, and to discover some wisdom they didn't know they had. Even a silly proverb may have a message lurking below the surface, despite the author's attempt to avoid it. Some students run into trouble when they think too hard about being profound; tell them to concentrate on the form and not worry too much about the content.

You can publish the best proverbs on a broadside or in a pamphlet called "The Class 5-304 Book of New Proverbs." Poet Harry Greenberg makes an annual trip to New York's Chinatown, where he buys a carton of unfilled fortune cookies; the students write their sayings on slips of paper, which they insert into the cookies and pass around, making for a popular session.

> Junkies are full of junk, winos are full of wine, but I'm full of pride.
> No boat will drown you.
> Thou who can't fight, shouldn't start; he who starts should get
>   punished.
> The sword can cut the pen.
> If you don't love animals, you don't love your parents.
> He who knows nothing must learn to know.
> Don't blame the cat for having kittens.
> He who is average can't get into a circus, and he who is a midget
>   will not get a job in the gas station.

People born underground know the truth about flowers.
Your weapon is your destruction.
Shooting the shadow does no good.
He who makes nonsense will make sense someday.
The clouds in the sky make the sun go down.

(some variations on an old favorite):

A wax apple a day keeps the doctor in pay.
An onion a day will keep everyone away.
A boat a day keeps the ocean awake.
                    — Various students (E)

If you don't like worms, don't be an early bird.
The curse of the living is to praise the dead.
He who speaks with forked tongue should not kiss a balloon.
                    — Students at Wagner Jr. High School

47
Slang and Style

Using the slang expressions, fashion styles, and fads of the day, a writer can capture the local color of time and place, and reveal character.

Slang

Carl Sandburg referred to slang as "language which takes off its coat, spits on its hands, — and goes to work." When used appropriately, slang can invigorate writing and bring the reader into the world of the story or poem. Slang expressions may exclude some readers, so writers should make sure that the gist of what is being said is accessible.

A freewheeling discussion of slang is fun and a good way to demonstrate that language is a living and lively, constantly changing ecosystem, allowing mutants and hybrids to have their day, and ultimately governed by the doctrine of survival of the fittest. Slang words and expressions (including slang definitions of standard words, such as "bad" meaning "good") lurk outside the "official" language; if they hang around long enough they are deemed worthy of public display in dictionaries, though with a label "slang" or "informal" (Samuel Johnson used the word "low") warning writers that using this word or phrase in formal discourse is equivalent to wearing blue jeans to a fancy restaurant. Many writers choose to wear jeans in their formal essays anyway. Some slang words eventually enter the lexographic pantheon without qualifiers.

When Eldridge Cleaver's *Soul on Ice* was published in 1968, *rapping* was parenthetically defined as "talking." Today, most readers are familiar with that usage, which you can find designated as "slang" in most dictionaries; however, it will take the next generation of dictionary editions to catch up with *rap* as in "rap records." H.L. Mencken theorized that slang terms survive when they provide a name for a new object or concept ("ghost writer") or are a "more succinct or more picturesque designation for something already familiar" ("killjoy").

Students should understand that there is no such thing as *the* dictionary. Dictionaries are written and edited, and they often take opposing stands on the acceptability of a word or phrase. *Bamboozle,* which goes back more than two centuries, is considered to be slang by the *Oxford American Dictionary,* while *Webster's New Collegiate* accepts it as a "real" word.

Discuss with the class slang expressions currently in vogue and ones they remember from previous years. In such discussions I become a student as the class patiently explains the latest vagaries of language, including new definitions of old words. I was distressed when a fifth grader informed me that I was an "old folk," but relieved when she defined an "old folk" as anyone over 21.

This excerpt from Wesley Brown's novel *Tragic Magic* shows how slang can flavor dialogue:

> "Before we continue," the disc jockey said, "I'd like to take a brief pause for the cause. And the cause this week for all you up-and-coming freaks is who can come closest to dressing like that baddest bone among the dry, the brittle, and the weary: Slick Swanson, disc jockey for WHIP. Now, we have our spotters on the floor to see who is sportin the meanest threads. And the one who is chosen will be freak for a week, courtesy of WHIP. So profile for a while, y'all, and remember that style is character."

Style

Slang expressions come in and out of fashion, as do clothing styles and fads. Expand your discussion of slang to include the ins and outs of fashions and activities, which are often accompanied by new jargon. This excerpt from Maureen Strange's novel *Beginners* deals with the language and styles of the early '60s:

> Bessie shuddered through her sophomore year. She was right... high school *was* different from junior high...it was worse! Much worse! How much more of this could she take? Through her years of waiting in the wings, waiting and hoping to be accepted by the neat, Bessie had witnessed their innumerable neat trends, neat fads, variations in neatspeak, neatdress, neatlook, and changes in basic neatbehavior and neatdemeanor that occurred more or less annually. Nobody truly neat would be caught wearing last season's colors (see *Mademoiselle* and *Glamour* "Fall Preview" issues: gold and brown replaced the previous year's royal blue; plum replaced the gold and brown; wine replaced the plum; olive green replaced the wine; and if you think you can pass off two years ago's plum as this year's wine, you've got another think coming); or last season's style (the knit cardigan replaced the pullover; the mohair replaced the knit; the alpaca replaced the mohair, etc.) or last season's hairdo (the artichoke replaced the bouffant; the flip

replaced the artichoke; the straight look replaced the flip, etc.) or using last year's put down ("I'm impressed" replaced "rank out"; *"you're cool"* replaced "I'm impressed"; "whoopee do" replaced *"you're cool,"* etc.). You could tell an unneat person a mile off because they were out of date. Neat people had a kind of neat radar, and when a new trend was set it spread immediately, as though there'd been a neat conference in the auditorium where the head neat person handed down the up-to-the-minute neat dictates which he'd acquired exclusively from some yet higher authority on what was neat, say, his brother who was a freshman at Brown. Suddenly every neat person you ran into would be acting in accordance with the new neat dictates. It made Bessie think of *The Invasion of the Body Snatchers;* you'd run into someone and as soon as you took a good look at them or heard their voice you'd know right away if they'd been gotten to, if they'd become one of *them.* One day Debbie came out with a perfectly executed, neatly inflected "whoopee do!" and Bessie thought "oh *no*...not my best *friend!"*

Write something emphasizing slang expressions and/or styles and fads. You might want to write an updated version of Maureen Strange's paragraph.

Being in the 8th grade is not all it's cracked up to be. The endless "Yo, man"'s and "Hey, baby" kind of get to you. "Far-out and heavy" is the joke now and to make fun of it, "Close-in and light" is used. Of course, "chilly-dogs" are now in — except in my book. "Ooo, la-la Sasson" went in with a bang and came out with a kick by "the Jordache look." I have to admit, the retarded "Hip-hops" have to be the worst. Can you imagine those "boxes" people carry around only play 10 songs that sound exactly the same? I mean, cool baby, let's face it! This city is real bad. (I mean bad as in bad not bad as in good — if you get my drift). "Crayons" are now in with see-through plastic jackets. Wo, man, this is it. People have to speak out about their language. And remember, "I mean, like hey man," use the language well. Roller skating is in. That's my bag. I mean, picking up those foxy fly-guys is just great! Get those rolling wheels going! Now you're chillin' out. I mean, "Sugar Bee" an' "Rocky Cee" have got the beat. Vicious, man! Jam-Jam Jimmy came in and I must have been the last person to know about it. Not that I care, but it's such a pisser when people say, "Man, you never heard of that?"

—Sherry Schwartz (M)

Make up new slang expressions.

You're pulling my root.
You're taking my mind.
You're singing me away.
You're running me out.
Hit the lights.

—Sloane Armstrong (E)

150

A discussion can revolve around the "buzz" words peculiar to specific sports and professions. Baseball pitchers, who used to worry about speed and control, now cultivate velocity and location. When Atari plays Apple in softball, do the pitchers attempt to access the plate with the ball in such a way that it doesn't interface with the bat?

48
Clichés

When I was 12, a friend got a letter that described the humidity in Florida with "You could cut the air with a knife." My friend repeated that phrase to me and said, "Now *that's* great writing." It *is* a fine image, but upon hearing it subsequently from other sources I began to doubt that my friend's correspondent had introduced it into the language.

Clichés are gems of figurative language that have been dulled by overuse. We've gotten tired of them, forgetting that they were once poetry or they wouldn't have become clichés. Poet Charles Simic has said, "The dream of every honest cliché is to enter a great poem." A new context can breathe life into a faltering phrase, but most clichés aren't so lucky, and are ignored by all but the most amateur and the most daring poets.

Discuss clichés with the class. Make a list of them on the board with your students, and then have each one read out loud, slowly. Ask the class to savor the words as if they were just entering the language, and to visualize the images.

Here's a list of clichés that are like fresh Broadway stars of decades ago now relegated to doing the same show over and over in summer stock:

> shattered like glass
> a broken heart
> quick as lightning
> wracking your brains
> he'll be back before you know it
> that takes the cake
> she's like a bull in a china shop

Students may not have heard of all these, and they may know some that you don't. Ask if students know clichés from other languages; are there English counterparts to them?

Write a poem with a cliché as the title, trying to find a new slant on it. I wrote this one using one of the top-ten clichés:

Love at First Sight

It was a novelty store, and I went in just for the novelty of it. She was in front of the counter, listening to the old proprietor say: "I have here one of those illusion paintings, a rare one. You either see a beautiful couple making love, or a skull. They say this one was used by Freud himself on his patients — if at first sight you see the couple, then you're a lover of life and love. But if you focus on the skull first, you're closely involved with death, and there's not much hope for you."

With that, he unwrapped the painting. She and I hesitated, then looked at the picture, then at each other. We both saw the skull. And have been together ever since.

Instead of using the cliché as the title, you can make it the last line, or put it anywhere else in the poem, attempting to make the cliché's dream of entering a great poem come true.

•

Write a poem that is chock-full of clichés. So many that you could choke a horse with them. More clichés than all the tea in China.

•

Combine two or more clichés to make a new one, such as: "It was so quiet you could hear a mouse drop."

49
Curses, Charms, and Insults

Words can affect as well as reflect the way people feel, as demonstrated earlier in the Power of Words assignment. Many primitive cultures believed that words could go beyond affecting opinions and emotions, that they could actually *effect* such physical results as healing, punishment, and agricultural success. The Navajo Indians so believed in the power of language that one was quoted as saying, "I have always been a poor man. I do not know a single song."

Literary uses of the magical power of words include Shakespeare's witches in *Macbeth* ("Double, double toil and trouble;/ Fire burn and cauldron bubble. . . By the pricking of my thumbs,/ Something wicked this way comes.") and Byron's Manfred, who beckons the spirits by imploring: "I call upon ye by the written charm/ which gives me power upon you — Rise! Appear!"

Curses, imprecations, incantations, charms, and magic spells are linguistic missives with more ambition than your run-of-the-mill couplet (although many love poems have been written with the objective of inducing behavioral change). Wishing upon a star will always have its share of young practitioners.

Write a curse, incantation, charm, spell, or wish-upon-a-star, anything to bring about a tangible change — for better or worse — or conjure the appearance or disappearance of anyone or anything. Here is an imprecation from a Quiché Indian in Guatemala (as quoted in The Gift of Language *by Margaret Schlauch):*

> Today I call on you, you cross of evil, and tell you this thing: So-and-so, a man who has money, he scorns me, and it gnaws at my vitals that he scorns me! Did I want anything from him? Did I want any of his money? Let

154

him have it and welcome! But today I bewitch him. . . . Let him feel it now! Mountain of witchcraft, cross of evil. I call on you. . . . I call on a rocky cliff, I call on an abyss, on the hollow tree, on the clump grass, on the thorn bush, on the wind and the clouds, so that he may see and know: I am a master of witchcraft!

Curse

Oh Magus Extraordinary, come to my aid, seek out the soul of the one who should not exist in happiness. Seraph, raise thee, burning all of her worldly possessions. Oh, Bechard, bring hail and tempests that follow her everywhere. Rangola, cause sickness and widowhood on all of those people about whom she cares. Oh, Mighty Set, come, come to my aid in the termination of her world so that I may again rest. With the spirits' aid, I curse thy name and all that you touch, even as far as the ground upon which you walk. You shall die 10,000 merciless painful deaths. You will regret forever the tampering of my power and mind. I curse thee.

— Laura Fisher (HS)

•

Insults

While actual imprecations are not prevalent these days, perhaps their modern equivalent is the insult, which can release anger and frustration without even reaching its object (as when the baseball fan in the last row of the bleachers diagnoses the optical ill health of the umpire and makes suggestions as to what he can do and where). Even the bluntest, most prosaic insults use figurative language ("Hey, ump, you bum, you stink; you blind or what?"). The "ranks" (short for rank-outs) we used when I was a kid included: "You'd have to look up to see down," "I rank you so low you could play handball on the curb," and "You could walk under a pregnant ant."

Witty insults are the basis of acts by comedians such as Don Rickles and Joan Rivers; even those who find this pair to be distasteful have probably chuckled at Groucho's ability to debunk pretension with a well-phrased zinger. Linguistic pacifists can laugh without guilt at Woody Allen, who aims many of his barbs at the most available target — himself.

Insults are not the exclusive province of bleacher hecklers, children rank-out artists, and entertainers; they have a long literary tradition as well. Poet Robert Burns (no relation to George) once called a critic ". . . thou pickle-herring in the puppet show of nonsense." Critics, of course, dish out more than they are dished; Alexander Wollcott served this one in a theater review: "The scenery was beautiful but the actors got in front of it. The play left a taste of lukewarm parsnip juice." (These and many other insults are contained in *The Book of Insults* by Nancy McPhee.)

Discuss insults with the class, and ask them to write down some insults they have heard and to make up some new ones.

Your eyes are the steam
from the kettle that opened
your mother's mail
revealing her secret lover
    — Tina Murray (HS)

156

50
Lists

A list of lists: laundry list; shopping list; things to do; great moments in history, sports, or show business; Christmas card list; a list of writing assignments.

Listing is a way of sorting out, storing, and quickly conveying information. Unencumbered by the demands of complete sentences and paragraphs, the writer can concentrate on content. Lists are streamlined and serve specific functions. Lists can be fun (Woody Allen used the form of the list for humorous ends in his short story "The Laundry List" in *Getting Even*), and can be a popular and profitable literary endeavor (*The Book of Lists* by David Wallechinsky, Irving Wallace, and Amy Wallace).

A fascinating list was submitted by James Agee as part of his application for a Guggenheim Fellowship in 1937. Agee listed, then annotated, more than forty projects he could work on, including:

Notes for color photography.
A revue.
Three or four love stories.
A study in the pathology of "laziness."
Stories whose whole intention is the direct communication of the
    intensity of common experience.
Collections and analyses of faces; of news pictures.
A new form of movie short roughly equivalent to the lyric poem.
The inanimate and non-human.
Analyses of miscommunication; the corruption of idea.
A notebook.

The remainder of Agee's list and the annotations are equally engaging and ambitious, but the application was turned down, which might make us feel a little less distressed about our own rejections — perhaps our rejectors are wrong, too.

Explain to the class that there are private foundations and government agencies that award money for research and creative work, provided you can sell them on your proposal. For the purpose of this assignment, we will create a new foundation: The Omnipotent and Benevolent Foundation for Giving Big Bucks for Almost Anything. Students should list projects they would work on if there were not only world enough and time, but also the money needed to buy world and time.

Projects can be in the arts, sciences, or humanities, or they can be personal ("track down my father and yell at him for leaving my mother, and then try to be friends with him") or humanitarian (a fourth grader proposed a shelter for homeless animals). No project is too ambitious or too frivolous.

Students can list several projects, and then elaborate on some or all of them.

•

Sei Shonagon was a court lady in tenth-century Japan. Her remarkable journal, published as *The Pillow Book of Sei Shonagon,* includes events of the day, descriptions of landscape and people, and social history. Featured in the book are 164 "lists"; some are straightforward topics ("Embarrassing Things," "Trees") and others are more elusive ("Things that gain by being painted," "Things that are distant though near"). The lists accompanying these topics blend the general and the specific, describing perceptions and experiences recognizable across the ten centuries and thousands of miles separating us from the author. Listed under the topic "Things That Give a Pathetic Expression" is "The expression of a woman plucking her eyebrows," and under "Adorable Things" is "One picks up a pretty baby and holds him for a while in one's arms; while one is fondling him, he clings to one's neck and then falls asleep." Here are some other list categories used by Shonagon, with examples:

> *Squalid Things:* The inside of a cat's ear. *Things That Give a Clean Feeling:* The play of the light on water as one pours it into a vessel; a new wooden chest. *Things That Have Lost Their Power:* A large boat which is high and dry in a creek at ebb-tide; a large tree that has been blown down in a gale and lies on its side with its roots in the air; the retreating figure of a sumo wrestler who has been defeated in a match. *Awkward Things:* One has gone to a house and asked to see someone, but the wrong person appears, thinking that it is he who is wanted — this is especially awkward if one has brought a present. *Things That Gain By Being Painted:* Pines, autumn fields, mountain villages and paths; cranes and deer; a very cold winter scene. *Embarrassing Things:* a man whom one loves gets drunk and keeps repeating himself; a man recites his own poems (not especially good ones) and tells one

158

about the praise they have received. *Surprising and Distressing Things:* All night long one has been waiting for a man who one thought was sure to arrive—at dawn, just when one has forgotten about him for a moment and dozed off, a crow caws loudly—one wakes with a start and sees that it is daytime, most astonishing. *Annoying Things:* One has sent someone a poem (or a reply to a poem) and, after the messenger has left, thinks of a couple of words that ought to be changed. *Things That Make One's Heart Beat Faster:* It is night and one is expecting a visitor—suddenly one is startled by the sound of rain-drops, which the wind blows against the shutters. *People Who Look Pleased With Themselves:* During a small-bow contest one of the archers coughs—the man who is about to shoot is distracted by the sound and becomes nervous, but he manages to control himself and his arrow shoots off with a loud twang, hitting the target—how pleased he looks with himself!

Here are some original list headings I have used with students:

Things That Cause a Letdown After Anticipation; Times When You Painfully Suppress a Giggle; Times When Someone is Right but You Get Mad at Them Anyway; Times When You Have to Take a Risk; Things One Is in a Hurry to See; Things to Write About; Things I Regret; The Best (Worst) Meals I've Eaten.

Students can make lists for these or their own topics. Another application of the *Pillow Book* lists is for students to write about a time when one of the situations Shonagon described, or something similar, happened to them.

Pillow Book Lists

Things that are comforting if you have sprained your soul:
a hot omlette with sharp cheddar cheese, fresh mushrooms and black olives—lots of hot cocoa and graham crackers;
anything by Mahler, played softly while you sit in front of the fireplace with your feet propped up on the hearth, watching the wavering orange inner-life of the coals;
Shakespeare's 29th and 30th sonnets.

Innocuous, inaccurate statements:
1. allow four to six weeks for delivery
2. "press down while turning clockwise" and other childproof caps
3. allow for minor shrinkage
4. jumbo shrimp
5. home-style cooking

Not-so-innocuous, inaccurate statements:
1. it's all in your head
2. satisfaction guaranteed or your money back

3. yield
4. pedestrians have right-of-way
                                    —Anne Larsen (HS)

Things that give a clean feeling:
        new, clean, starched sheets after a day of work.

People who look pleased with themselves:
        person with a mug of tea by a fire on a winter afternoon.

Things that give pathetic impression:
        a dog shivering on doorstep;
        a squirrel with non-furry tail;
        someone having trouble with a task you can easily perform.
                                    —Kathryn Lambert (HS)

Surprising and distressing things:
        realizing your little brother is two inches taller than you (and two
        inches stronger), thus finding out the hard way you can't pick
        on him anymore.

Things that have lost their power:
        the engine of a '68 Chevy;
        the heart of an 86-year-old woman.

Things that make you smile inside:
        watching someone eat crackers.
                                    —Tina Murray (HS)

   The function of list assignments is to help students crystalize perceptions and convey concepts sharply with few words. Lists work well with
students who have writing problems, because lists are less intimidating than
open-ended stories and poems. Point out that lists make for good notebook
entries, and can generate material for future writing.

51
Place

While Senator Bill Bradley was a college basketball star, he was profiled by John McPhee for *The New Yorker*. As they were talking on a basketball court, Bradley nonchalantly flipped the ball over his shoulder without looking at the basket; it went through the hoop. Bradley explained that on the court "you develop a sense of where you are." The same goes for writers.

The importance of place varies from writer to writer, from piece to piece; sometimes setting is in the foreground, while other times it's barely in the background. Fiction writer Erskine Caldwell found that place dictates action: "I would have nothing to write about if the people of the story had no fixed place of living. . . a fixed place for people rules the lives and conduct of the characters."

Legendary editor Maxwell Perkins, in a letter to novelist Marcia Davenport regarding her manuscript for *East Side, West Side,* wrote: "New York is a foremost character in the novel. . . . Make Jessie more aware, as she goes about in cars, cabs and afoot, of the way New York is, of how Fifth Avenue looks in the haze of afternoon. . . . The reader must be aware of time and place, as it is and as she remembers it. That is what you intended, and means only an occasional reference to give a sense — by sight or smell or whatever — of a spot of New York."

Although many poems and stories exist out of time and place, others have one or more settings, and students should have some practice in using setting as a resource. I sometimes tell a student who has written a story lacking "a sense of where you are": "It can happen anywhere, but it should be *some*where." A sense of place is conveyed by the descriptive details, comparisons, and dialogue you choose to present.

Ask students to notice how filmmakers aquaint the audience with a setting by selecting where and for how long to aim the camera. Both close-ups (which emphasize details) and long shots (which provide context) can be effective. The camera can linger on a wall grafitto, then pull back to a long shot as two characters cross the street, so we can see the traffic (a good way of telling time as well as place).

A scene-setting shot in filmmaking is referred to as an "establishing shot." The movie "West Side Story" opens with an aerial view of the New York City skyline, then pans the slum where the action will transpire, and zooms in to a close-up of fingers snapping. Another approach would have been to start with the close-up and then pull back.

Film techniques are useful for writers, who can think of themselves as looking through a camera as they write about a place. In a story, an "establishing shot" paragraph can set the scene before the action starts, or vice versa. For example, a story might open with a description of a Broadway theater, then focus on a dancer. Or, it can start with the dancer, and then reveal to the reader that we are in a theater.

As characters talk and move, the writer should consider whether there's anything about where they are that would enhance the reader's feel for the scene. Should you pull away from the characters and focus on setting? Remember that you can show readers things that a character doesn't see or notice, or you can limit yourself to showing settings exclusively through the eyes of a character, depending on the point of view you choose.

•

Here are two models for writing about a place: a poem by Robert Bly about driving through the Midwest, and excerpts from a prose piece by Osip Mandelstam about Moscow; both places are treated as living organisms. Bly uses light, sound, and personification to evoke a mood of tranquil motion, solitude without alienation. Mandelstam shows Moscow as a city of conflicting images.

Before you read these to the class, emphasize the importance of visualizing the images projected by the language. As you read, the students should *be there*. Then reread one or both pieces, asking students to concentrate on the *language,* perhaps jotting down words or phrases that help them get to know the place.

Driving Toward the Lac Qui Parle River

I
I am driving; it is dusk; Minnesota.
The stubble field catches the last growth of sun.
The soybeans are breathing on all sides.
Old men are sitting before their houses on carseats
In the small towns. I am happy,
The moon rising above the turkey sheds.

II
The small world of the car
Plunges through the deep fields of the night,
On the road from Willmar to Milan.
This solitude covered with iron
Moves through the fields of night
Penetrated by the noise of crickets.

III
Nearly to Milan, suddenly a small bridge,
And water kneeling in the moonlight.
In small towns the houses are built right on the ground;
The lamplight falls on all fours in the grass.
When I reach the river, the full moon covers it;
A few people are talking low in a boat.
                              —Robert Bly

•

I know you, Grand Opera Square — the navel of European cities....
I walk out from the dusty oasis of the Metropole — a world hotel —
where I have wandered in under the glass marquee through the corridors,
streets of an internal city — stopping now and then in front of the ambushes
of mirrors, or resting on the quiet inner lawn with its wicker chairs and bamboo benches — out onto the Square, swallowing sunlight like a blind
man....
    ...It's a cold summer. It is as if a bag of ice, which is simply impossible to melt completely, were hidden in the deep green of the Neskuchnovo,
its chill crawling through all of web-footed Moscow....
    You don't love the city if you don't appreciate its rags, its humble,
miserable sections; if you haven't panted on the staircases, gotten tangled in
tin cans, in the cats' miaowing....
    You don't love the city if you don't know its petty habits: for example, a cab never climbs the hump of the Kamergerskovo without a horse
ahead and the beggars and flower-girls following behind....the flower-
sellers walk off to one side and spit on their roses....
    During a thunderstorm it's good to sit in Trolley A, tearing through
the green waist-band of Moscow, running after the storm clouds....More
and more white bones of houses are sticking clear out. Against the leaden
slabs of the thunderstorm you see first the Kremlin, white bird boxes, and
last the insane stone card game of the Educational House, an intoxication of
plaster and windows, regular as honeycombs, piles of shapes that have no
dignity....
    ...and the city begins to shape itself, already it can't stop, and it piles
up like rising bread dough, storey after storey....
    I love the banks, menageries of money-changers, where all the
cashiers sit behind bars like dangerous beasts....
                              —Excerpts from "Cold Summer" by Osip Mandelstam,
                                              translated by Eve Shapiro

163

Write about a place. There can be people in it, but they should be treated as no more or less important than any other part of the scenery. If appropriate, include movement, emulating the motion picture rather than the still photograph. Use words and images to make the place come alive; be specific and direct, supporting generalizations ("nice," "beautiful," "scary"). Use sounds as well as sights; snippets of dialogue can be included.

I grew up in the town of St. Joseph, a pit-stop off the highway which ran from Minneapolis-St. Paul and beyond. It was a small, Catholic town, tucked off in its own little space of Minnesota. There was a peculiar stillness in the air, so naive and constant, it couldn't have been true.

One road ran down the center of the town like the backbone of a fish. Vertebrae of neat, little houses with carefully trimmed lawns ran parallel to it. Towards the end of the road the church stood across from the three grocery stores which took turns having sales, and the bakery and the post office. A gas station stood at the very end of the road, or the very beginning, depending on your direction.

The nucleus of the town was St. Benedict College, an all-girl Catholic college where my father taught German. I once found a beautiful statue near the cemetery. It was of the Virgin Mary with eyes so sad and real. I could never find it again.

Old, brick buildings rose like castles above the shaded campus. I spent long hours wandering the woodchip paths leading through walls of rose bushes. They were like walls of brilliant, cool fire when they bloomed. I always pulled myself in when I passed through for fear of the thorns. At the end of one path there was a goldfish pond. The goldfish were flashes of quick-copper among the bullfinch and plush greenery.

It was a magical place for a child to own.

—Lenore Hammers (HS)

•

"Place" refers to indoor as well as outside settings. Max Jacob, in *Advice to a Young Poet,* writes with admiration for the way Poe used an indoor setting in "The Raven": "There is a lamp, an armchair of violet velvet, a bust of Pallas, a night of meditation and study. See how the decor is arranged for maximum effect. What a model! You need to know what effect you want to produce and set out everything with that effect in view." I should point out that sometimes the writer is not sure what effect he or she is striving for until the scenery fills in. Like anything else, scenery is open to revision.

Inside a House

Describe a tour through a house or apartment, either your own or another person's, real or imagined. You can look inside medicine chests, drawers, and closets. You might find some interesting things squirreled away in the attic or basement; even the garbage might hold something revealing (journalist A.J. Weberman wrote an article based on what he found in Bob Dylan's garbage). You might imagine that you are a detective or reporter assigned to find out everything about the place. Here is an excerpt from Scott Spencer's novel Endless Love, *in which the protagonist searches through his parents' cabinet:*

> I ran to the bookcases and opened the sliding cabinet doors at their base: folded tablecloths; aqua and burgandy burlap napkins from Mexico; a few old copies of *The National Guardian;* a chessboard and a White Owl cigar box for the chess pieces; dozens of little boxes of delicate pink birthday candles; boxes of checks; boxes of unsharpened pencils; a portable sewing kit, housed in heavy, shiny paper and decorated by a drawing of an elephant waving its trunk. . . .

Here's an excerpt from a story by a high school student:

> Then she went into the bedroom. There were more plants and books and posters. The dresser, chair, and floor were covered with Copenhagen after-shave, a deck of scattered cards with a building on the back, coconut oil, a tube of Prussian Blue and Naples Yellow oil paint, rolling papers, a bent guitar transposer, and a pile of dirty clothes in the corner. Everything was bathed in a shimmering ultra-violet haze coming from one corner near the two mattresses on the floor, which had blankets and sheets haphazardly falling off them to the wood floor. . . .

•

Place is particularly important in genre stories: a creaking castle during a thunderstorm; the sun beating down on a vast yellow plain as hoofbeats get louder from the horizon; a plush drawing room, where the maid comes across a spot of blood on the beige carpet and screams when she sees what's been dragged under the couch.

Write a scene-setting paragraph for a genre story: horror, science fiction, western, mystery, romance, or adventure. Or, write a fragment of a genre story that goes against the grain: a love story that takes place in a haunted house, or a gothic horror story occurring amidst cowboys on a serene desert.

•

Playwrights precede their scripts with a description of the stage setting, sometimes in elaborate detail; Tennessee Williams' settings read like parts of novels. Write a stage setting for a play.

•

Neighborhood

Students often have a hard time writing about their neighborhood, perhaps because our senses become blunted to that which is most familiar. These two approaches make it easier:

Write about your neighborhood at a specific time (early in the morning, after school, Saturday afternoon).

Write five separate lines about your neighborhood, with each line containing at least one concrete detail or comparison.

Other familiar places you might ask students to write about are the lunchroom, playground, and after-school hangouts.

52
Architectural Designs

I got the idea for this assignment while looking out a classroom window as students were filing in. I had looked at that view many times before, but this time I noticed something that announced itself as a writing assignment.

What I observed for the first time was: nothing. Amidst the dense city, where buildings lean against one another, there was an empty lot. It had been empty since the beginning of the school year.

I set aside my plans for the session and asked the sixth graders to join me at the window and look across the street. "What do you see?" I asked.

"Nothing," they replied.

"Good, now put something there."

I asked them to design a use for that space, to make an architectural rendering in words. The design could be fanciful or practical; it could be an apartment building, school, playground, discotheque, park, or a combination. Students could use all or part of the space, and money was no object. They could describe the inside and/or outside of any structures.

If there is no empty space nearby, ask your students to imagine one:

If that building across the street were to be torn down, what would you put in its place?

You can take this idea much further by putting together a unit on architecture and design, with students creating their own model town, doing drawings or sculptures to accompany their writings.

> First I'd have the bricks in red and orange. Then I'd make three bedrooms. The house would be pretty big. One bedroom for me, one for my mother and father and one for my brother. I'd have a private room for anybody who wants to talk on the phone. A disco room for music and danc-

ing only. And a family room that has T.V., games, etc. I'd have a kitchen with turning drawers, and cabinets. An air freshener. A room downstairs for experiments. We'd have a room for our animals — dog, cat, etc. A bathroom in every bedroom. A closet stacked with candy and all kinds of sweets for special occasions or any time you want a snack. There would be no mice or bugs. My house will be so neat they will be afraid to come in. There will be a tennis court, pool, a volleyball court. And a big yard so beautiful that rabbits and squirrels won't be afraid to COME HERE!

— Veanda Martin (E)

53
Night

Night evokes poetry, perhaps because darkness corresponds to our unconscious and awakens dreams. Or maybe it's because sundown brings the end of the routine for most people, and veils our surroundings in mystery. Night can enchant or frighten.

Things go bump in the night; moonlight inspires lovers and lunatics; "merry wanderers" roam Shakespeare's midsummer night; "In the real dark night of the soul it is always three o'clock in the morning" (Fitzgerald); "It's a marvelous night for a moondance" (Van Morrison); "The poet now and then catches sight of the figures that people the night-world — spirits, demons, and gods" (Jung).

Discuss the night, its physical and psychological components.

Write about the night:
1) *A mood piece, describing a place at nighttime.*
2) *Someone's dark night of the soul.*
3) *The journal of a "merry wanderer" of the night.*
4) *Choreograph a "moondance."*

A Night Time Person

As the bright lamppost light dies down and the black night sky takes over, we only have the stars to give us light.

Then the flowers stop dancing to sleep and the wind begins to blow as though it's looking for something that it's lost.

Maybe what it's lost is me.

Maybe it's looking for me because every night it bangs on the shutters and pounds on the door trying to get in.

Sometimes the wind gives up and blows a cool breeze which puts me to sleep, bringing dreams of adventures, mysteries, and scary things to seek out, or rainbows, rooms of crystal, kids helping old people cross the street.

The night time seems like you're reading a book and you are the writer of the book.

—Maggie Haberman (E)

In the Dead of the Night

The dead of the night
Reminds me of when the light would burn bright
It reminds me of birds when they fly
Very high in the sky

It reminds me of crowded houses
And all the hanging clothes

All the people in the library
And all the secretaries
my father doesn't have

It reminds me of a sitting chair
And all the ladies in their windows bare

It reminds me of running cars
And all the people in all the bars.
—Jordan Jones (E)

54
Things

We often have complex relationships with inanimate objects. This excerpt from Patricia Hampl's story "Look at a Teacup" starts with a description of the teacup which evolves into a metaphor for her mother:

>   The cup is thin — you can almost see through its paleness when it's empty; right now, there's tea in it, and its level can be gauged from the shadow outside. The cup is the palest watergreen imaginable. Sometimes, in certain lights, it is so pale it doesn't seem green at all, just something not white. It is shiny, and there are thin bands of gold around the edges of the saucer and cup, and again midway down the bowl of the cup and at its base, which is subtly formed into a semi-pedestal. There is also a band of gold on the inner circle of the saucer, but it has been worn away, after so many years, except for a dulled, blurred line. There is no other decoration on the outside of the cup — a bland precision of lines and curved light.
>   But inside the cup there are flowers, as if someone had scattered a bouquet and it had tumbled into separate blossoms, falling in a full circle around the inside. Some have fallen faster to the bottom of the cup, while some are still floating. The blossoms don't seem to be pasted on the surface like decals, they really appear to be caught in motion. And now, for the first time, alone in my own house (I've never been alone with one of these cups before; they were her company dishes), I see that no two flowers on the cup or the saucer are the same. Each a different flower — different colors, different attitudes of falling, nothing to create a pattern. Yet the cup and saucer together are pure light, something extremely delicate but definite. As refined as a face.
>   My mother's face, which has fallen into sadness.

This prose poem by Laura Gilpin about a cherished object is more concerned with function than appearance:

My Great-Grandmother's Wristwatch

My great-grandmother's wristwatch still keeps perfect time. My mother said, as far as she can remember, it's always kept perfect time, when her grandmother had it, when her mother had it, and when she had it. But a few years ago it stopped and none of the jewelers she took it to could fix it. They said it was too old and they didn't have parts for it. My mother saved it for sentimental value and it sat around the house for a couple of years.

Then she gave it to me because I needed a watch and she said I could have it if I could get it fixed. Most jewelers wouldn't even look at it, it was so old. Finally in New York I found a watchmaker who specialized in antiques. He cleaned and polished my great-grandmother's watch and now it looks as good as new. He said it's a fine piece of machinery. He said it just needed some adjustments. He said it works perfectly. He said it should last another lifetime.

Write about an object, including physical description, memories involving the object, and why the object is important to you.

My grandma owns a victrola that still works. It was her mother's, and by now it's very valuable. It's square and has a big, shiny horn, and you crank it up.

Sometimes when she listens to it, my grandma gets depressed because it reminds her of her mother. She listens to her old records and smiles and relaxes. She's very gentle with it, because she is afraid it will break.

My grandmother really doesn't use any modern resources, because she believes that the best way to do anything is to do it by hand.

—Leah Carlson (E)

•

Imbue an object with "mystical" qualities, as high school student Deirdre Kovac does in this poem:

Shoes

Shoes know how a closet breathes at midnight
and can return the kiss of long dresses and corners.
Their arches never taste the odor of wet earth,
the glassy sound of snow,
or the worn leather of linoleum.

Shoes fear laces
that twist violently,
binding the shoe closer to itself.

172

A shoe's one desire is to lie alone,
tongue down in the sand,
letting its sole soak in the sunlight.

Write a story in which an object plays an important part. The object can be the clue to a mystery or a key image in a character's life, like the "Rosebud" sled in Citizen Kane.

55
Both Sides of the Coin

News reporters may strive to be objective — to present situations as they are — but it is virtually impossible to describe an event without some subjectivity resulting from the reporter's decisions as to what to include and exclude, and the language used. Photography is considered by some to be intrinsically objective ("the camera never lies"), but even a photograph of an apple is suffused with the photographer's point of view via variables such as lighting, angle, and background. Poets and fiction writers — who function without the constraint of even theoretical objectivity — may choose to let an event "speak for itself," but the reader gets a translation of what the writer "hears" the event saying.

Opinions and feelings are better expressed through figurative language and selection and arrangement of information than through judgmental harranguing. Subjective writing can be done overtly — using blatantly loaded words — or more subtly, with the trappings of objectivity. Students can understand how language colors subject matter by writing about one topic in contrasting ways — in effect, presenting both sides of the coin.

Two people can have the same experience but have opposite things to say about it. One writer may re-create a wonderful night of camping in the woods, including the sensual delights of a thunderstorm, while a companion writes about a miserable, sodden night of disorientation and the horror of the unknown. A film character portrayed by Peter Lorre says, "I love digging up graves at midnight; it's exciting." His poem about the "objective" stimuli would differ greatly from mine. The way we experience the seasons is open to interpretation: Ingmar Bergman's bleak film "Winter Light" does not depict its characters "walking in a winter wonderland."

These excerpts from D.H. Lawrence's poem "Bats" present one side of the coin and refer to the other:

> .... Bats, and an uneasy creeping in one's scalp
> As the bats swoop overhead!
> Flying madly.
> ....
> Little lumps that fly in air and have
> voices indefinite, wildly vindictive;
> ....
> Creatures that hang themselves up like an old rag to sleep
> And disgustingly upside down.
> Hanging upside down like rows of disgusting old rags
> and grinning in their sleep.
> Bats!
> In China the bat is a symbol of happiness.
> Not for me!

Ask students to note the loaded words that tip the scale against bats in this poem ("uneasy creeping," "madly," "lumps," "wildly vindictive," etc.). Then ask the students to imagine that they have the Chinese point of view of bats as a "symbol of happiness" and create images that depict bats in a positive light.

The Bat

You hang upside down —
a small, brown, fuzzy burst of life
curled in a frightened ball
after frenzied flight,
breathing heavily —
tiny ribs heaving
through sheer skin wings
folded over your small chest.
Your eyes are closed;
when opened they are like
small stones —
shiny, clean, and sparkling....
— Gerry Pearlberg (M)

Write about any situation, object, living being, place, or experience, showing first one side of the coin, then the other.

School

That big ugly prison.
Reaching out with scaly hands

to pull you into its horrid cage.
Chains of books and pencils
with a teacher's desk at one end
and you on the other.

The lovely red brick palace
and friendly shouts of pals.
Your teacher to greet you
and your own desk to sit at.
A nice pencil and a piece of paper
to guide you.

— Sebastian Bacchus (E)

Frogs

The gruesome little creatures
with warts all over their bodies.
Hopping and making disgusting
little croaks as if they are saying
gimmee this gimmee that.
Waking people up in the middle
of the night and murdering the
nice little flies.

The cute little things
with beautiful shiny green skin
hopping to the edge of
a lake to dip their petite bodies.
After they have their swim
they wait to catch the flies
and eat them
so the flies won't overpopulate.

— Anya Regelin (E)

On Stage

The beady little eyes staring at me, a small, feeble performer. Everyone fixed at me, their sharp mouths, their need for excitement, their antennae hair twisted with boredom. I can already feel the tomatoes being thrown at me in my tutu. The seams seem to tear, I feel my nakedness, everyone laughing with anxiety. My instructor screaming foul language and insults at me. There will be no hope.

The wonderful time has come to perform for an audience of assorted friends, relatives, and strangers who have come to see *moi*. Practicing my steps with glee. Backstage, hopping, skipping, singing, dancing around. Me in my tutu, a solo dance, everybody will be cheering, whistling, applauding for more. Their eyes watching every move I make. The eyes — brown, black, hazel — watching a pink silhouette on stage. I am confident. I feel the roses, the carnations, etc., being thrown at me. My instructor crying with happiness. There is hope.

— Michelle Barkowski (E)

176

Write about war as a romantic adventure and as a horrifying nightmare.

Write about what it's like to be very young (on one side of that coin, adults often cater to your needs and don't expect you to work, while on the other side you can't — or adults won't let you — do what you want to do).

Being Small

Being small is a pain in the neck. I know you get a lot of attention but you get it even when you don't want it. All these people pinching your cheeks and kissing you with their mushy lips and saying, "Are you a good girl?" Coochi, coochi, coo. I hate that, who needs it. I can't even go anywhere because I'm supposed to be defenseless. On top of that, I get no privacy, everyone looks at me when my diapers are being changed. When I get hit everyone laughs because they see my little red behind. But there's one good thing about it. When I do something bad, I don't get blamed, because I'm only a baby and I didn't realize what I was doing.

—Melissa Rivera (E)

•

Write a dialogue — or interior monologues — for two lovers, siblings, or a parent and child who see things differently.

56
Looking Back on Today;
Looking Ahead to Tomorrow

Vladimir Mayakovsky wrote about the need for writers to distance themselves from their subject matter in order to gain perspective. "It's a good idea," he said, "to begin writing a poem about the first of May in November or December, when you feel a desperate need for May." As a substitute for distance in time, Mayakovsky recommended a change in scenery: "Substitute a change of place for the slow passage of time, and in the space of one day you literally pass over centuries, in imagination."

I can't offer students a change of place, but I do suggest that they use their imaginations to travel through time, in the following assignment:

Imagine yourself as an adult looking back on your childhood (or adolescence). *What survives in your memories of when you were eleven years old* (substitute current age of students)? *When you look back, what makes you smile or cringe?*

This shift in perspective sometimes works wonders in unlocking the wealth of material students often ignore because it is so close to them. Imagining that they are telling stories to their grandchildren is another premise that gives students a reason to write.

Each Monday at 4:30 I would ring her doorbell, apartment 4A, Pauline Styler; I always called her Mrs. Styler. The stout little lady with curly red hair—when I was 11, I was already taller than she was.

We would practice on her grand piano. Her living room was all blue except for the piano. She always wore flower printed blouses. I would sit on the stool and she sat on my right.

We started with scales. Up and down the piano. It sometimes became tedious. The same eight notes ringing in my head. If I did well (which was rarely), she'd compliment me. She then cheerfully said, "On to the more complicated stuff." She always sounded so eager. No matter what I did wrong, the notes, beats, or just messed up, she would find something nice to say.

She taught me how to practice slowly. If she hadn't taught me this, I would not be able to play one piece all the way through. My piano teacher was a terrific piano player. She could look at a piece and play it. This sometimes made me mad. I planned to play as well as she could.

Oh those songs, those beautiful songs. How long ago were those songs flowing through my fingers. I wonder, are those songs still flowing? Or have they become part of my memory, singing on my teacher's grand piano?

—Kathy Yen (E)

•

After having the students see themselves from the future, assign this natural follow up:

Write about where you are and what you are doing twenty years from now. Visualize your appearance and actions. One approach is to write about a typical day, including home and/or work. Present the material directly, as if it is actually happening now. Use the present tense.

Compare the following two paragraphs. The first one is *about* being a doctor, whereas in the second the writer *is* a doctor.

In 20 years I think I will be a doctor. If there is an emergency of some sort, they would call me in the middle of the night. I would answer the call and feel satisfied because being a doctor means I could help people.

•

The ringing reaches into my sleep and pulls me awake. 4:20 AM "Dr. Swanson, this is Southside General, we have an emergency here—auto accident." I squint into the light and my eyes adjust as I put my clothes on. I am fully awake when I lean over the patient's body and check the vital signs. . . .

179

57
Being Alone

Discuss with the students how they feel about being alone. What do they do? Where do they go? Do they release inhibitions by acting in ways they wouldn't while someone is watching, like the persona in this William Carlos Williams poem?

Danse Russe

If when my wife is sleeping
and the baby and Kathleen
are sleeping
and the sun is a flame-white disc
in silken mists
above shining trees, —
if I in my north room
dance naked, grotesquely
before my mirror
waving my shirt round my head
and singing softly to myself:
"I am lonely, lonely.
I was born to be lonely,
I am best so!"
If I admire my arms, my face,
my shoulders, flanks, buttocks
against the yellow drawn shades, —

Who shall say I am not
the happy genius of my household?

This is not a lonely lament, but rather a celebration of joyful solitude by a man for whom being alone is a luxury. Dancing by himself, he is a "happy genius" with no one to judge, interfere with, or inhibit him.

Discuss attitudes toward being alone, and the predicament of feeling lonely even though you are not alone. Talk about the places students go to be alone — hiding places, places where no one will bother them, etc. — and what they do, think about, and feel there.

Being Alone

When I'm alone
I go to the smallest room
where the curtains fly.
When I'm alone
I turn off the light
and sit in my favorite
chair by the window.
The gentle breeze blowing
in my window onto my face.
I think of many colors
being put together
and slowly separating.
I feel calm when I'm alone.
Not being disturbed, just thinking.
It's like going into a deep sleep.
The door slowly opens
my mother comes in and
turns on my light.
I wake up from my deep sleep.
I'm no longer alone.

— Janet Gary (M)

58
Life and Death

Writers often fail when they attempt to deal with large, general issues. It is usually preferable to start writing about something specific and let the subject matter expand, perhaps via metaphorical implications. I would never have planned to ask kids to write about "life and death," but might have encouraged them to write about a piece of cheese or fresh fruit as it changes from day to day, or a specific birth or death, perhaps of a pet. And yet, I inadvertantly gave such a general assignment, and it worked.

Sixth grader Nancy Arnold asked me for an idea; I was distracted, en route to another student, and blurted out teasingly, "I don't know.... Write about the wonders of life." I really meant that I wanted her to come up with her own idea. A few minutes later, feeling that I had been flippant with her, I returned to give some serious help. But she was writing busily and shooed me away. Later, she handed me this piece:

Life and Death

I've heard that... Life is a bowl of cherries. You live, then each one is eaten which means death. Life goes on endlessly, until—the wonders of your mind get eaten like a bowl of cherries. Baby, child, teenager, adult, senior citizen—The last cherry is you. The wonders of your mind are too old to remember the times when you were young. Life is...That's what the world needs, a definition of life. The wonders of your mind get rusty. Slowly, slowly, the cranks stop turning, the wheels stop going and a little man comes down from your brain to your heart and says it's all over, bub. Then you float in the air. Feeling numb. Not thinking. Floating, twisting, turning. Now it's not so smooth. It's rough. Things going through your mind—CRAZY, DREAMING, ZOOM, ZANG, ZING, STOP. It comes to an end. You feel a large thump. You fall, never to move again. You, the cherry, have gone into heaven's stomach.

There was something about the phrase "wonders of life" that set this in motion. I read it to the class, and it inspired other "life and death" poems. Classmate Alex Omura wrote an extended metaphor.

Life is an iron bridge.
It will be slowly built.
At the right moment,
when it is finished,
it will be unveiled.
All sparkling, new and strong.
It will grow in fame,
and more and more be used.
It will sway in storms
and come out the same.
Now and then it will need
a new paint job,
or a girder will be repaired,
but that won't affect it much.
As it grows older
more and more people
will depend on it.
Its personality will be
more and more known.
One day the first signs
of rust will be discovered.
It can't take
all that it used to.

Slowly it will rot
and eventually be closed down.
Finally it will collapse,
but a new bridge
will be built
with the broken pieces.

•

Many adults find death to be an uncomfortable subject to discuss, perhaps because it was hushed up when *we* were kids. This is unfortunate because when the subject is treated openly, children are able to write about death with insight, feeling, and sometimes humor.

Occasionally I read to students poetry dealing with death, especially when the subject comes up in the students' writings or classroom discussions. I might say, "I've noticed a few of you have been writing about deaths in your families, or the loss of pets you felt close to, or situations you read or heard about. Would you like me to bring in some examples of how other writers have dealt with this subject?"

After a reading of such material, and a discussion of the various literary approaches to the subject, I give students some time to write, if they choose, about death.

59
Loss

The Ball Poem

What is the boy now, who has lost his ball,
What, what is he to do? I saw it go
Merrily bouncing, down the street, and then
Merrily over—there it is in the water!
No use to say "O there are other balls":
An ultimate shaking grief fixes the boy
As he stands rigid, trembling, staring down
All his young days into the harbour where
His ball went. I would not intrude on him,
A dime, another ball, is worthless. Now
He senses first responsibility
In a world of possessions. People will take balls,
Balls will be lost always, little boy,
And no one buys a ball back. Money is external.
He is learning, well behind his desperate eyes,
The epistemology of loss, how to stand up
Knowing what every man must one day know
And most know many days, how to stand up.
And gradually light returns to the street,
A whistle blows, the ball is out of sight,
Soon part of me will explore the deep and dark
Floor of the harbour...I am everywhere,
I suffer and move, my mind and my heart move
With all that move me, under the water
Or whistling, I am not a little boy.
                    —John Berryman

"The Ball Poem" deals on the surface with the loss of a ball by a little boy. Another ball may be put in its place, but nothing can replace that particular ball, into which Berryman has rolled all material objects as well as the act of growing up.

The more we live, the more we have to deal with loss, a subject that occurs frequently in literature and will turn up in student writing whether assigned or not. (Teenagers often write about lost love, younger students about lost pets.)

Objects

Discuss the loss of objects, such as toys, articles of clothing, notebooks, etc., then ask students to write about an object they have lost — either through their own fault or because it was taken from them. You can narrow the field by providing the following stages, although not all stages will apply to every case. Remind students that they can fictionalize. You might want to include pets in this category.

1) **Description of the object.** *This should convey the sense of value and attachment you feel for the object.* Good background is the Things assignment (chapter 54).

2) **The moment of loss.** *You discover that the object is missing. What emotions do you feel? There is likely to be a sequence of emotions, such as disbelief to shock to anger to sadness.* Students should draw on their experiences with the Emotion assignments (chapter 18).

3) **The period of adjustment.** *This might include acceptance of the loss; moments forgetting that the object is lost, then experiencing the loss all over; and nostalgia for the lost object.*

4) **Replacement.** *Is the object replaced by another of the same kind, or does something else take its place in your heart? What does the new object have that the old one didn't, and vice versa?*

You can make this into a Lost and Found assignment by adding a reunion with the object (which might reveal that the person has changed in the interim).

People

The above stages can be adapted to the loss of people. The ultimate loss is through death, but we lose people in other ways, too. We lose friendships, love relationships, and parents (through divorce). Some losses are scheduled: students "lose" their teachers, camp counselors, and others who come into their lives to serve temporary roles.

60
Appreciation

Sentiments like "You never miss the water till the well runs dry" or "You're sure gonna miss me when I'm gone" are as true as they are common. Who has not waxed nostalgic for the "good old days" and even felt twinges of longing for some bad old days as well?

As Carly Simon sings, *"These are* the good old days," yet how often do you look around you and savor the things you appreciate, things that may be different or gone tomorrow?

I silently scanned a fifth grade classroom for a minute and said, "I'm looking at you closely because I'll never see this again." A student asked, "How come you're not coming back to the school?"

"I am coming back," I replied. "I'll be here next Wednesday, but you won't be the same. Why not?"

We quickly established that they would all be wearing different clothes, and someone might be absent (or have moved), etc. I told them to look out the window—that scene, too, would change by next Wednesday. Some leaves would be more colorful, and others would be gone.

"This is your last year together in this building," I said. Some cheered, but they were starting to get the pont: in a few years they would be saying, "Remember when we were in fifth grade?" I read them this poem by Tomas Transtromer, translated by Robert Bly:

The Open Window

I shaved one morning standing
by the open window
on the second story.

Switched on the razor.
It started to hum.
A heavier and heavier whirr.
Grew to a roar.
Grew to a helicopter.
And a voice—the pilot's—pierced
the noise, shouting:
"Keep your eyes open!
You're seeing this for the last time!"
Rose.
Floated low over the summer.
The small things I love, what do they amount to?
So many variations of green.
And especially in the red of housewells.
Beetles glittered in the dung, in the sun.
Cellars pulled up by the roots
sailed through the air.
Industry.
Printing presses crawled along.
People at that instant
were the only things motionless.
They held their minute of silence.
And the dead in the churchyard especially
held still
like those who posed in the early days of the camera.
Fly low!
I didn't know which way
to turn my head—
my sight was divided
like a horse's.

In light of our discussion, the line "You're seeing this for the last time" was comprehensible. I wrote one of Transtromer's lines on the board: "The small things I love, what do they amount to?" Under it I wrote "Things I Didn't Know I Loved," the title of a poem by the Turkish poet Nazim Hikmet, who spent many years as a political prisoner. I read these excerpts, in English translation by Randy Blasing and Mitlu Konuk:

From **Things I Didn't Know I Loved**

it's 1962 March 28th
I'm sitting by the window on the Prague-Berlin train
night is falling
I never knew I liked
night descending like a tired bird on the smoky wet plain
I don't like
likening the descent of evening to that of a tired bird

I didn't know I loved the soil
can someone who hasn't worked the soil love it
I've never worked the soil
it must be my only Platonic love

and here I've loved the river all this time
whether motionless like this it curls skirting the hills
European hills topped off with chateaus
or whether it stretches out flat as far as the eye can see

*   *   *

I didn't know I liked the sky
cloudy or clear
the blue vault that Andrei watched on his back on the
    battlefield at Borodino
in prison I translated both volumes of *War and Peace* into Turkish

*   *   *

I didn't know I loved flowers
friends sent me three red carnations in prison
I just remembered the stars
I love them too
whether I'm floored watching them from below
or whether I'm flying by their side

*   *   *

snow flashes in front of my eyes
both heavy wet steady snow and the dry whirling kind
I didn't know I liked snow
I never knew I loved the sun
even when setting cherry-red as now
in Istanbul too it sometimes sets in postcard colors
but you aren't about to paint it like that

*   *   *

I didn't know I loved the clouds
whether I'm under or up above them
whether they look like giants or shaggy white beasts

*   *

I didn't know I liked rain
whether it falls like a fine net or splatters against the glass my heart leaves
me tangled up in a net or trapped inside a drop and takes off for un-
charted countries I didn't know I loved rain but why did I suddenly
discover all these passions sitting
by the window on the Prague-Berlin train
is it because I lit my sixth cigarette
one alone is enough to kill me
is it because I'm almost dead from thinking about someone back in
    Moscow
her hair straw-blond eyelashes blue

189

the train plunges on through the pitch-black night
I never knew I liked the night pitch-black
sparks fly from the engine
I didn't know I loved sparks
I didn't know I loved so many things and I had to wait until I was sixty to
find it out sitting by the window on the Prague-Berlin train watching the
world disappear as if on a journey from which one does not return

19 April 1962 Moscow

*Write your version of "Things I Didn't Know I Loved," imagining
that you have been separated from your current surroundings and now appreciate things more than you did before.*

As I sit by the window I concentrate on the falling rain. Each drop
bringing me back in time, to a small room, dark with no lights on because
electricity is expensive. My grandmother sitting by the window knitting
wool sweaters for the oncoming winter. I never realized how comforting it
was to hear the sound of her rocking chair going back and forth, back and
forth in beat with the raindrops. My grandfather smoking his pipe in the
corner, exploring the possibilities of expanding the form. My mother stands
near the fireplace cradling my little brother in her arms. Her face distraught
with thoughts of the past. I know she must be thinking of my father. He left
a few years ago — two years, three months and four days to be exact — said he
couldn't put up with the family anymore.

I can see his point. Mom is very devoted to grandpa and in this house
he is in charge. I guess dad couldn't take it. I can understand why he left but I
can't forgive him. I remember he used to hold me and tell me stories, give me
piggy back rides on his back. I remember he used to comb my hair after I
took a bath and tell me that one day I would wear golden bands and precious
gems.

There was a very small kitchen, containing just the essentials — sink,
refrigerator, stove, and a table. The paint on the ceiling was peeling over the
stove, and the faucet would drip. The carpet was worn, where we used to
walk from the livingroom through the kitchen out the back door. There was
a little hole at the side of the door. We once had a mouse who resided there.
That's when we got our cat, before my brother was born. Then my father
left, the cat was gone one morning, and so was the mouse.

My grandmother and grandfather are both dead, my brother no
longer a child in my mother's arms. And me looking back to the past, seeing
things I didn't see the first time, reliving them again, appreciating what I had
and wanting it back now. The rain continues to fall.

— Toni Ann Del Grasso (HS)

•

*Using Transtromer's phrase, write a poem called "The Small Things I
Love."*

190

(You can substitute "appreciate" for "love" in either assignment. Include annoyances that you might miss if they weren't there.)

•

Another possibility is suggested by the helicopter ride in "The Open Window," in which the persona, having taken an imaginative leap into the helicopter, flies over his surroundings:

"Fly low" over your life and "keep your eyes open." Write what you see. Include yourself—alone or interacting with others—in your daily routine, going to your favorite places, etc. You can also travel back in time and write about your past as if you were actually seeing it.

> I fly low
> Soaring like a bird
> I see my life
> I begin to understand
> My family
> My friends
> The bullies
> The disasters
> The unhappiness
> All that I know.
> Those few parts
> of my measly life
> Seem extraordinary to me now.
> All that I cherish
> I seemed to disregard.
> Now I value
> Just one thing.
> This whatever
> Whoever
> This life I live
> Now.
>   — William Arnold (E)

•

A way of approaching this subject area with younger students is to ask them to write "What I Would Miss If I Moved."

61
Inventory

Store owners take inventories from time to time in order to keep track of what they have and what they need. All of us should set aside all other business occasionally and take stock, reflecting on what is happening in our inner and outer lives: dreams and possessions, family and friends, agendas and accomplishments. The classroom may or may not provide the "tranquility" Wordsworth might have needed for such an assignment, but ask students to write an Inventory poem. This is one of mine:

Inventory 1981

Each year I make more money
and my purchasing power decreases.
In this I am not alone.
Still, I have managed to acquire recently:
a watch, camera, answering machine,
coffee maker, shirts, and sweaters.
I wonder how I got along before.
Sex is less important,
or rather, it's more important
so I do it less.
Strangers call me "Mr." — nothing new
but I no longer pause before answering.
My family has suffered no losses.
My sister has added two;
I, none.
I am in love but we are not together,
which is, I suppose,
better than the opposite.
I have accepted as fact that

I will never catch up with work
but most things get done eventually;
also, that summer is not as long
as the rest of the year,
so expectations must be adjusted accordingly.
I worry less about colds and the flu,
more about cancer and heart attacks.
I am 34
and so is everyone else
in my high school and college classes,
though they can't all say
as I can
that they weigh the same now as then.
I don't get the desire as often
to grab someone by the shoulders
and say, "Listen to me, look at me,
don't you *understand?"*
But when I do,
it's sadder when they don't.
At 16, Wordsworth wrote about
"dear delicious pain."
At more than twice that age
I no longer think pain is delicious,
though some is palatable.
I no longer open my pores to everything
simply because it's *there,*
but when I do,
I drink long and deep.

62
Writing from Visuals

Visual images, such as photographs and paintings, have been widely used in writing assignments, but the writing can turn out dull when students do litle more than "caption" the pictures: "This is a photograph of a man and a woman. The man looks happy. He is wearing a suit. The woman looks sad. She is wearing a dress."

Write from inside the picture; "enter" the image and get the feel of the territory around you. You can write from the point of view of a person or object in the picture; you can inject yourself into the scene and see what effect you have on the picture; or, you can write a dialogue between participants.

This poem by Gregory Orr dramatizes the concept of "entering" the image:

The Room

With crayons and pieces of paper, I entered the empty room.
I sat on the floor and drew pictures all day.
One day I held a picture against the bare wall:
it was a window. Climbing through,

I stood in a sloping field
at dusk. As I began walking, night settled.
Far ahead in the valley, I saw the lights
of a village, and always at my back I felt
the white room swallowing what was passed.

Another approach:
Think of the picture as a freeze-frame in a movie: what has happened

194

to lead up to this moment, and/or what will happen next?

These approaches can be used in a writing/art project. Have students do their own drawings (you can ask for interesting characters in exotic settings, or just let the students draw on their own) and ask them to treat their drawings as above. Student photographs can be used in the same way.

63
Music

Music can be used as a background while writing. Novelist Jerzy Kosinski says that the driving quality of rock music injects energy into his writing. Poet John Ashbery listens to a classical radio station to provide him with an ambience, and the commercials and announcements "get sucked into the poem, as do all kinds of things in my immediate environment. . . ." I listen to all kinds of music. Other writers find *any* music to be a distraction. On rare occasions, if a class wants it, I'll allow music in the background as long as it aids rather than impedes writing.

For this assignment, music moves from the background to the foreground; students "translate" musical sounds into language, or at least let the music inform the writing. I use selections of instrumental music that I think will be evocative and provocative, favoring John Coltrane, Mahler, Tchaikovsky, and the solo piano work of Keith Jarrett and Chick Corea, to name just a few. Sometimes I choose music with a quickly changing landscape; other times I pick a piece with a sustained mood (such as the fourth movement of Mahler's Fifth Symphony). Ballet scores lend themselves to narrative development.

This is my set-up:

You can tune in and out of the music, alternating listening and writing, or you can write and listen at the same time. You can do freewriting as the music plays, without trying hard to be influenced by the music, or you can try to stay as close as possible to the mood of the music. You can close your eyes and let the music form "pictures" in your mind, and transcribe the mental images onto the page, thinking of the music as the soundtrack for a movie being screened by your imagination. If the music inspires an idea, you can leave the music behind and go with that idea.

196

You might try to do with language something akin to what the musicians are doing with sound: listen to the way the sax player reaches almost beyond his grasp for a note—perhaps he is unsure of what he is reaching for—then grabs a soaring note and holds onto it. See if you can grab a word or image that you didn't know was there.

You might come up with a series of images or a narrative.

Don't "think" too much, not even about the things I have just said.

For many students, music conjures up images and narratives that extend beyond what they have previously written.

Piano

A small baby is gurgling to itself quietly
and so delicately.
Rain trickles outside repeatedly.
Getting softer I listen more carefully.
The baby is up and crawling in her crib.
The faucet is dripping.
A cloud floats by the window in slow motion.
Baby falls asleep and is motionless.
She kicks her leg and finally is asleep again.
— Chrissy Keller (E)

a ballet dancer dancing on the sidewalk in ragged clothes.
a poor, graven image tap dancing on a plastic see-through floor.
mirrors surrounding it, confusing and sad, grey and now and then
        there is light.
twisting again, flowing by like a river unreal, but it's there—coming
        at you and falling back now.
smooth and fast.
a dark dank place—then there is light again.
running through a meadow and falling and rolling down to a well.
splashes of color on a desolate painting in the midst of a fog.
castle towers above the mist and angels peering down and giving light.
running around a bend and speeding back again.
very confused, trying to escape.
running in circles, a dog after its tail.
a sturdy oak tree that's an image of a boat on a misty sea.
opening and closing, all together in one.
into a painting and out again.
afraid, and huddling in a dark, cold attic.
sensing danger, now and again.
— Kyra Bromley (E)

Improvisation

Most jazz musicians begin a piece by stating the melody, following it with improvisations, and ending with a restatement of the melody. Some musicians improvise close to the melody, while others go so far afield they

197

would need a passport to get back to the tune. Play the students an example of musical improvisation, telling them to raise their hands each time they hear elements of the melody.

Write a few lines of poetry and then improvise off the language and ideas in those lines.

Melody:
Time's a wastin',
gotta get out. Into the world
of space. Stars floating lightly by.
Singing a song of praise to the Sun.

Improvisation:
The Universe having a square dance
in slow motion. Then I, ME myself
and I sing the song of happiness
to the sun. In tribe
the notes flow in and out.
Time is plenty. No need to run.
But still go into the world of
space. Stars floating heavenly by
singing a song of praise to the moon.
The universe having a waltzing
movement in slow motion. Then
my friend, sing a song of gladness
to the moon. In the clan the
notes flow in and out.
              —Lisa Burris (E)

•

Even on the remotest outskirts of the avant-garde, crumpling a piece of paper would hardly be called a musical performance, but just a couple of seconds of crumple can evoke imagery leading to sustained writing.

Poet/teacher Kenneth Koch has used the piece of paper as a simple musical instrument in his classes, and I tried it with a group of sixth graders I had been working with for over a year. These students needed very little to get them going, and this was about as little as I could give them. I told them to close their eyes and pay careful attention; they would hear a sound and should write down anything the sound inspires. Minimal external stimulus would trigger an internal impulse. I told them not to tell me what the sound actually was, and they could go far away from the sound.

Crackle. I unfolded the paper and played it again, even though no one had called, "Encore!" *Crackle.* These are some of the instant images:

A crackling fire
Shuffling through the woods on fallen brown leaves
Me in a bathtub getting pruned
My bones cracking in odd places
When my brother gets real mad and hits the table in anger
Doing the dishes, because I hate doing the dishes and the sound reminds
    me of anger and hate
A building being torn down
After wrapping a present, then stopping and jamming a piece of tape on
    it to fasten it

    I asked the students to turn these sparks into flames, and several good stories grew from the simple act of squishing a piece of paper.

64
Writing/Art Projects

The confluence of the visual arts and writing can propagate exciting work that not only sharpens skills in each area but also demonstrates how the juxtaposition of words and visual images can deepen the impact of each component. (Dave Morice treats this subject in *How to Make Poetry Comics,* published by Teachers & Writers.) The following projects can be taught in collaboration with the art teacher, or by yourself.

Seasonal Calendar
Each year, dozens of new calendars compete for a chunk of the Christmas gift budget, depicting wildlife, cats, cars, breads (with recipes), literary figures, and the latest Star Wars and Muppet characters, sometimes accompanied by captions that you never get around to reading. Painter Barbara Siegel and I were working with a fifth grade class and decided to have the kids publish their own calendar. Financial restrictions determined that we divide the calendar into seasons rather than months (not the first artistic decision to be influenced by money).

I asked the students to write one-liners about each season. They could write as many as they wanted, or they could write longer poems with the understanding that single lines would be excerpted. Meanwhile, Barbara worked similarly with visual images, asking the students to work small so that we wouldn't have the expense of reductions. We typed the best lines and cut out the best visuals, and arranged them horizontally into seasonal collages — interspersing the written lines with the drawings — on 8½ x 11-inch pages. Each page of art and writing would be attached to a page containing the days and dates of the corresponding three months, which we took from a published calendar.

The following is the layout pattern, developed by poet/printer Larry "Mr. Excitement" Zirlin; all layouts are horizontal, and should be printed or photocopied on cardstock (very thick paper): The front of card No. 1 is the cover (designed using transfer type); the back of card No. 1 is the word/drawing collage of winter. The front of card No. 2 contains the calendars for the winter months; the back is the collage for the spring months. The front of card No. 3 contains the calendar for the spring months, backed by the summer collage. The front of card No. 4 is the calendar for the summer months, backed by the fall collage. The front of card No. 5 is the fall calendar, backed by a page for credits.

After the cards were printed, we punched holes at the centers of the tops, and tied each set together with yarn. Thus, when we flipped over the cover, the calendar was ready to be hung on the wall. (If you do this project, make sure that you provide the printer with a "dummy" of the printing pattern, with each page clearly labeled. Otherwise, it might be Christmas at the beach at your school.)

This was the written material for the calendar:

WINTER: rich snow and poor snow; hat messes up your hair; throat feels like it was eaten; snow so bright that when all the lights go out it guides you through the night; put on a sweater and a big ugly coat—looks like you're going to war; so cold put foot on radiator.

SPRING: a dream wakes up from a long sleep; smell the fresh woods of the trees; all the animals rip and run; flowers pop out of the ground like Bozo; flowers begin to dance to the music of the birds; explore new things in the forest.

SUMMER: a time for everything but coats; sometimes not a sound—but the sea; sad deep inside because I can't swim; pick a flower or pick a hobby; children hear the man call Ice Cream Ice Cream; go to White Castle or McDonald's and eat outside.

AUTUMN: summer is over, the pool is closed; here comes the hay fever sneeze: school and rain; shopping stores start to get warmer; something doesn't like the leaves; help find homes for animals.

•

Masks

A couple of years after our calendar project, Barbara Siegel and I were working separately with a sixth grade class. One morning as I was speaking to the class, I noticed a row of masks that the students had made by garnishing heavy construction paper with an assortment of materials, such as yarn, wires, and scraps of cloth. I asked the students about this gallery of bizarre countenances that was silently, but, it seemed, judgmentally observing my presentation. They explained that, working with Barbara, they had designed their masks as medieval characters, and they introduced me to the King, the King's Guard, Mad Doctor, Mad Doctor's Slave, Jester, Fool, Evil Devil, and the others.

We decided to give voices to these faces. Students were not restricted to writing about their own masks. One by one, students modelled the masks, parading around the room in character, while the others took notes.

The students wrote mask poems, which were, depending on their interpretations of the characters, clever, violent, diabolical, sweet, complaining, bitter, and bragging. Each author then read his or her poem out loud, while another student wore the mask and mimed the character. Barbara and I took a few students to the auditorium, where she accompanied their performances on piano. One girl put her poem to music and sang it a capella.

You can develop this into a performance project to be presented as an assembly or on tour to individual classrooms.

> I am the mad doctor.
> I used to be a regular doctor
> but one day a patient came in for a gall bladder operation
> and I gave him a brain transplant and he died.
> In court, where I was being tried for malpractice,
> they asked me why I gave the wrong operation
> and I told them that I had done a gall bladder the day before,
> and I didn't want to get in a rut.
> They said I was insane. How would *you* feel doing
> gall bladder operation after gall bladder operation?
> Besides, I like to tear
> and maul and destroy! How else will I realize my dream
> of becoming a worker in the Post Office?
> Anyway, they put me in Bellevue, but I escaped.
> I decided to get revenge
> by really being a mad doctor. I prayed to become insane
> and finally I did. Then I started
> making monsters out of people.
> King Kong was Shirley Temple until I got to her.
> Godzilla used to be Richard Nixon.
> Sometimes I wish I could help people,
> but when I think of my time at Bellevue
> I get angry and I'm glad I'm a mad doctor.
> Besides, I do help! Where would Hollywood
> be without Bigfoot?
> — Pamela Schwarzmann (E)

(For other Writing/Art projects, see Everything But the Book, Advertising, Greeting Cards, Writing from Visuals, and Invent a Magazine.)

65
Missing Links

Missing links may shorten a chain but they can expand the effectiveness of language. "Monkey see, monkey do" is stronger than "What a monkey will see a monkey will do." For this assignment, students write a series of words or short phrases with a minimum of filler. Each word should be carefully chosen, making this an exercise in selectivity and economy, and a good word-diet for students with a verbosity problem. Many poets use sentence fragments, and this assignment gives students some experience with that style.

There are two approaches. One method is to write in full sentences and then edit down. The other is to go straight to sparseness, writing slowly, editing in the mind. This example of the former process shows how a piece can gain strength through reduction.

> I go to sleep but I'm still tired. Then I realize I have a fever. I know I do because I cannot feel anything. It's so nice out, a summer day. I am frustrated because I am sick.

Less is more in the revision:

```
sleep      tired
           fever
know      cannot      feel
        nice     summer
frustrated     sick
              — Allison La Chapelle (E)
```

As you can see, the white space of the page is part of the poem. This one was written in one draft:

Jazz Piano

    fast   waves   fancy   high   tone   breathe
loneliness;   sad   smooth   slow   soft   mixtures flowing
    Lost   can't stop   crying for help   wonderful
soundalltogether
                    — Jennifer Perez (E)

In this example, sixth grader Jeannine Budihas created her own form, writing in columns:

It's cold   it's lonely
the stones   the sadness
the people   the ghosts
the boxes   the coffins
the accident   his death

204

66
Two Situations

What follows are two kinds of situations that exude tension, conflict, and sometimes humor.

Anywhere but Here

In *Hamlet,* Rosencrantz and Guildenstern lose their lives by allowing themselves to get into the wrong place at the wrong time. Tom Stoppard's *Rosencrantz and Guildenstern Are Dead,* which retells *Hamlet* from the point of view of these doomed bystanders, closes with them on a ship, on their way to deliver a message which includes their death warrant. Rosencrantz, upon discovering their predicament, says, "There must have been some point, somewhere, when we could have said, 'No.'"

We all find ourselves in situations when we'd rather be almost anywhere than where we are. We may get ourselves into such situations by being passive (as did Rosencrantz and Guildenstern); by chance (you enter a subway car and notice that everyone looks like they are auditioning for the Heavy role in "Friday the 13th Part 13," or you go to a party where you didn't know "this kind of stuff would be going on"); or by ignoring or not noticing warning signs (a little voice inside you says, "You're going to regret accepting this invitation to the Satanic Cult's Open House and Bake Sale").

Sometimes there is little or no choice, as when children are forced to accompany their parents to Aunt Smooch and Uncle Pinch's house. Other times, it's for your own good (you are in a raised swivel chair, your mouth laden with instruments, and a stranger with a drill is coming closer, closer). In all of these situations, you look around and say to yourself, "I-do-not-want-to-be-here."

Write an anecdote or story about this kind of situation. Concentrate

*on the surroundings and the ways your character reacts internally and exter-
nally. If you write about another person making you uncomfortable, you
can write a follow-up piece from the point of view of that person.*

One day my parents decided to go visit my grandparents, who try to
be nice but don't do so well. They pinch my cheeks, pat me on the head and
mess up my hair, and they go hysterical about everything. My grandmother
is always singing weird songs I never heard in my life and she is an awful
singer. And they're always saying, "Why don't you wash the dishes?" Then I
can finally go someplace I want, but I can't say no to them. Every time I visit
them they take me to the same place over and over and it is so boring I would
like to just disappear.

But they do a lot of nice things, like they take me to the movies and
give me candy and listen to what I have to say and they are very loving and
affectionate. Soon my parents say, "Come on, we have to go." I wait a little
and think, then I say, "Okay," and I leave with the door closing behind me.

—Cyris Sink (E)

•

It Wasn't Funny at the Time

On the stage, screen, and printed page, physical or psychic pain often
makes us laugh. It's all right to laugh at the slapstick comedian's topsy-turvy
encounter with a banana peel, but not at an old person's fall on the street,
though sometimes we have to supress a giggle when viewing a painful or embarrassing situation. (It was lip-biting time when one of my high school
teachers, furious at the class, admonished us to "Ship shape or shape out.")
We often laugh when recalling predicaments that weren't funny at the time
("You should have seen us when the police arrived....").

*Write about an incident that seems funny in retrospect, or about a
time when you had to hold back a laugh (such as when dad tried to assemble
the new bicycle and got greasy and frustrated and began to shout).*

206

67
Crime and Punishment

Life is full of crimes and punishments not involving lawyers and judges. Children are subject to the judicial systems of their parents: "You came home after curfew, therefore you cannot watch television this weekend." When kids mete out punishment to each other, it may not be as civil or explicit; "I'll get you for that" is a common open-ended threat of punishment.

As we get older, our punishments tend to be more oblique, with the punisher perhaps not fully aware of the punishment: "You hurt my feelings last night, so I am not going to return your next phone call, and I will be distant when you call back, and you won't know why." Overt revenge can take on violent dimensions, as any moviegoer or follower of the news can attest to.

The basic format for this assignment is: "For the crime of . . . . you are hereby sentenced to . . . ." The "crimes" students select can be real or fictitious transgressions, for which they mete out inventive punishments that could be collected into the Code of Ridiculous and Sublime Justice. Caution students that this is an exercise in *conceptualizing* extra-legal justice; the results are certainly not to be acted out.

Consider whether to make any restrictions on whom they can "punish" — whether, for example, teachers and parents should be off limits. Since children are usually on the receiving end of punishment from adults, this might be a good opportunity to let them have the upper hand. On paper.

Crime and Punishment

From my parents to me:
For not cleaning your room, we will keep the dryer on for a month while you sleep.

To my brother from me:
For going in my room and breaking my stereo, pulling out the plug on my clock, taking my letters and calligraphy set and stashing them in the freezer; last but not least, eavesdropping on my phone calls: I sentence you to take a long hot bath and wash your hair three times and wash your face with soap.

— Sherry Schwartz (M)

For the crime of the boys in the class calling me names, not nice names, such as "flatty," I sentence them to write the word "flatty" 1,000,000,000 times until they get sick of it. In addition, I will make them all run around the shopping center without anything on so people could tell them how ugly and skinny they are.

— Laura Frigo (M)

For the crime of hitting my cat, my brother gets to stick his head out the window while the bird droppings are falling down.

— Anonymous

68
Crazy

Perhaps mental illness is satirized and joked about because it is so frightening; we whistle in the dark of the unconscious. Insanity has also been treated seriously by filmmakers ("Through a Glass Darkly," "David and Lisa") and novelists *(I Never Promised You a Rose Garden),* and in a seriocomic way in such books as *One Flew Over the Cuckoo's Nest.*

Artists can be distinguished from crazy people—when there *is* a distinction—by their ability to discern between their creations and reality; to an insane person, surrealism is day-to-day reality. An artist may write about a lover who does not exist, but wouldn't take him or her out to dinner.

There are many ways of writing about this powerful and evocative subject. This is one approach to narrowing the field:

1) Write the activities and thought processes of someone on a day which culminates in commitment to a mental institution. You can write in the first person—perhaps as a diary entry (as Gogol did in "Diary of a Mad-man")—or in the third person. Your tone can be serious or satirical.

2) In the same manner, write about a day in the institution, including what is being done for (or against) the patient—such as therapy and medica-tion—and contact with other patients.

3) Write about the person after release from the institution. How has the experience affected your protagonist? (This could be reflected in a change of "voice.") How does he or she now relate to the world, including the circumstances that led to his or her problems.

Not only is this an opportunity for students to deal with a com-plicated and powerful topic, but it is also good practice in character trans-formation, one of the most important ingredients of fiction.

69
Diseases and Neuroses

So many things can go wrong with the human body and psyche that it's a wonder we hold together at all. Students in a mischievous mood can make up or identify even more physical and mental aberrations. If they are feeling charitable, they can prescribe cures.

Brow Furrows

Symptoms: Deep lines in the forehead and often around the mouth and eyes. Often the eyes are also afflicted with dark circles beneath the lower lids.

Cause: Pent up anger and/or anxiety, usually aggravated by exhaustion.

Common victims: People with tendencies to internalize tensions are the most susceptible. This disease is especially rampant among students.

Warning: This disease can be harmful, or even fatal, if left untreated. A ten-hour sleeping period can often lessen the symptoms, but a temper tantrum preferably directed at a wall, door knob, or another neutral object is often necessary. The throwing of pillows is highly recommended. After this original breakdown, it is essential to redirect this energy into productive channels. A prescription of friendship is essential to prevent a relapse.

—Lenore Hammers (HS)

70
Rules and Regulations

While looking through a fourth grader's folder, I came across a draft of regulations he planned to propose to the student government, including:

Don't touch any displays.
No pencils in the bathrooms.
No knives.
No throwing toilet paper at the ceiling.
Always have a lunchroom partner.
Everyone keeps their assigned seats.
No screaming in the halls.

After being presented by the district administration with proposed dress regulations for teachers, Leonard Davenport of the Lynbrook Teachers Association made a tongue-in-cheek counterproposal that included:

In order to reflect the professional status of the employee, the district shall provide smocks to all employees, freshly starched and rolled each morning at least ten minutes before the official start of the student day. Smocks shall be returned thirty minutes after student dismissal.

Students shall only see smocks in positions of authority and will learn to respect the smock as a symbol of the educated person.

Untenured smocks shall bear a yellow stripe down the back to show respect to the principal.

A smock shall be retired upon retirement of the respective teacher.

Richard Hugo in *The Triggering Town* has a "Nuts and Bolts" section, in which he presents suggestions for writers in the form of rules because he finds "the axiomatic tone preferable to a lot of qualifiers." Here are some excerpts:

> Use number 2 pencils. Get a good pencil sharpener and sharpen about twenty pencils. When one is dull, grab another.
> Don't erase. Cross out rapidly and violently, never with slow consideration if you can help it.
> . . . . Never *want* to say anything so strongly that you give up the option of finding something better. If you *have* to say it, you will.
> When you feel a poem is finished, print it. The time needed to print a word is a hair longer than the time needed to write it. In that extra moment, you may make some lovely changes. . . .

Write serious rules regarding any facet of school, home, or civic life, attempting to make the rules direct and precise. Or, draft "surrealist rules," either to make a satiric point or just for the fun of it. (In Woody Allen's film Bananas, *the leader of a Latin American country orders that underwear be worn* outside *the clothing and be changed every half hour.) The third option is to take a subjective area (such as writing, friendship, or love) and issue suggestions cast in Hugo's axiomatic tone.*

Rules and Regulations

Make the stanzas look balanced in some way. Never make the reader feel he's driving a coughing car unless you have a specific purpose for doing so.

Make the sentences clean. Kill any little obnoxious words which act as a bone in the person's throat. Sentences should flow smoothly, not bump over obtrusive words.

Paper is important. Just as you must love what you write with, you must love what you write on. For me, it was once college-ruled paper that was rounded on the edges.

Never write lying down. It tends to become uncomfortable, and then it gets distracting.

I used to only be able to write with a pencil that was slightly waxy, so it doesn't go dull so quickly. Now I love black or red Bic pens. It doesn't really matter what you write with, as long as you're in love with it.

— Lenore Hammer (HS)

71
Rituals

Holidays, ceremonies, and traditions contain rituals that are loaded with symbolism, costume, and metaphor, making them ripe subjects for a unit of writing assignments (which can supplement curricula such as the study of other cultures).

Discuss rituals that occur on Halloween, Christmas, Chanukah, and New Year's Eve, and at weddings, graduations, confirmations, and Bar Mitzvahs. What are the typical ways people dress, behave, and speak on these occasions? Students should try to look at these rituals freshly, through the eyes of the proverbial visitor from another planet. Ask the students to write briefly about one of these ritualistic occasions, suggesting that the writing concentrate on what can be seen and heard, lest it lapse into homilies and abstractions. If you have students from other countries, ask them to describe rituals from their homelands.

Tell the class about a wild ritual from the Middle Ages called the Feast of Fools. Here's a description of it from *A Distant Mirror* by Barbara Tuchman:

> An integral part of life, religion was both subjected to burlesque and unharmed by it. In the annual Feast of Fools at Christmastime, every rite and article of the Church no matter how sacred was celebrated in mockery. A...lord of the revels was elected from the inferior clergy...whose day it was to turn everything topsy-turvy. They...played dice on the altar and ate black puddings and sausages while mass was celebrated in nonsensical gibberish; swung censers made of old shoes emitting "stinking smoke"; officiated in the various offices of the priest wearing beast masks and dressed as women or minstrels; sang obscene songs in the choir; howled and hooted and jangled bells while the "Pope" recited a doggerel benediction....

This is a "gift event" from the Kwakiutl Indians, as adapted by Jerome Rothenberg in his anthology *Technicians of the Sacred*. Notice the playful tone.

Gift Event II

Start by giving everyone different colored glass bowls.
Have everyone give everyone else a glass bowl.
Give away handkerchiefs and soap and things like that.
Give away a sack of clams and a roll of toilet paper.
Give away teddybear candies, apples, suckers and oranges.
Give away pigs and geese and chickens, or pretend to do so.
Pretend to be different things.
Have the women pretend to be crows, have the men pretend to be something else.
Talk Chinese or something.
Make a narrow place at the entrance of a house and put a line at the end of it that you have to stoop under to get in.
Hang the line with all sorts of pots and pans to make a big noise.
Give away frying pans while saying things like "Here is this frying pan worth $100 and this one worth $200."
Give everyone a new name.
Give a name to a grandchild or think of something and go and get everything.

Create a new version of a traditional ritual, using your personal vision or your perception of cultural changes. Or, create a new ritual. Your ritual can be serious, or as bizarre as the Feast of Fools.

A New Wedding

You walk up the aisle with your father. The priest starts saying, "Do you BLA, BLA, BLA" and all that other junk. You say you're not sure and decide half an hour later. Then your about-to-be husband says, "Maybe," after the priest asks him to be your husband. He decides about half an hour later. Then the priest says to kiss everyone else but the one you just married. You start kissing everyone, even the priest, but your husband. Then you walk down the aisle with your high school boyfriend.

Instead of going on a honeymoon with your husband you go on the honeymoon with your high school boyfriend for a whole year. Your husband goes on his honeymoon with his high school girlfriend for a year. So both of you don't see each other for a year. When you come back you rent an apartment for just yourself. He rents an apartment for himself. It's far away from yours. You can date anyone you want and so can your husband.

As the years pass by both of you have a happy marriage by yourselves. Without even getting a divorce!

—Isabel Feliz (E)

214

Total Union Day

A day of rejoicing
Everywhere
Small Towns
Big Cities
New York, London, Paris, Beirut.
On this day
Everyone is one
Americas, Europe, even Asia.
Just One
Everybody in one country
The Earth.
Millions of tourists are pushing
In the Capitol City
New York.
The building
U.N. Building
The Time
12:00 noon
The Cry
We're *ONE*

                  —Michael Sid (E)

Evolution Day

      I woke up on a Sunday morning. I was quite excited because I knew that it was Evolution Day. The idea of this day was to act like a primitive ape when the day began, then slowly work up the evolutionary scale until we were superior beings at night. And this was my first chance to experience it because I had moved to the U.S.A. only 9 months ago. . . .

                  —Sam Nisson (E)

Personal Rituals

      Closer to home are the little rituals and traditions that develop in our private lives. Discuss the behavior and conversation patterns that evolve in families, with friends, or in school: things that happen somewhat predictably, such as the traditional pileup for use of the bathroom in the morning, and the ritualistic preparations for going on vacation. Parents can be asked about rituals from their childhood. (A ritual from my mother's childhood that did not bridge the generation gap was that each Friday she would find a live fish swimming in the bathtub: Saturday's dinner.)

      Ask the students to write about personal rituals. This assignment not only gets students to examine material from their daily lives, it also gives them practice in creating atmosphere—such rituals can flavor subsequent stories.

215

Our Trip to South Carolina

We have done this for so long as I can remember: ride in the car 14 hours nonstop except for gas and bathrooms. We play the same games everytime: "The Guessing Game" and "Who Am I?" Both games are pretty much alike but we were bored so we named them separately.

My mother always packs a picnic lunch. About 12 o'clock we eat. But I eat differently than everyone else. I eat very slowly, nibble by nibble. When I'm done with the meat I lick off the mayonnaise (I don't like mustard) very slowly. When I'm done with that I eat the bread very slowly nibble by nibble, bit by bit. I'm done. No more and another 10 hours to go.

— Anya Regelin (E)

"Julie!"

"What do you want?" I ask.

"Did you put the cap back on the toothpaste?" my dad asks.

"Yes," I say and then I run to the bathroom to cover it. Too late! There is my dad standing over the sink, his muscles bulging and his arms crossed. Uh oh.

"I thought you put the cap back on."

"Uh, so did I," I say.

"Well, next time you better do it. Or else." Then he takes me by the neck, his warm hands against me, and tickles me to death.

— Julie Hiraga (E)

72
Occasional Poems

The impulse to write often comes from internal rumblings and inter-personal relationships — we place our private lives into the public arena. But we often overlook public events and situations as possible subject matter. Poetry written about a specific occasion or event — including such semi-public events as weddings, funerals, and birthdays — is called "occasional poetry." For this assignment, I include poems of social and political commentary that are not pegged to a specific occasion.

Storytellers, poets, and minstrels have always had their say about what was going on; when printing became accessible, writers began distributing topical poems and ballads on broadsides. In *The Uses of Poetry,* Denys Thompson cites a 16th-century poem "against a profiteering land-lord, who had turned out a widow to use her house as a corn-store." Milton, Wordsworth, and Yeats wrote occasional poetry (Milton wrote political sonnets, a form previously reserved for love themes), as do contemporary poets such as Allen Ginsberg, Robert Bly, and Carolyn Forché.

In the 1960s, topical songwriters such as Phil Ochs, Tom Paxton, and Bob Dylan wrote on subjects ranging from the Vietnam War to the death in the ring of boxer Davey Moore. Their songs, including Dylan's "Oxford Town" (about the integration of the University of Mississippi) and Ochs's "I Ain't Marching Anymore," were sung at rallies, galvanizing emotions and actions. The following poem was written by one of my sixth grade students, who read it at an anti-nuclear rally in Central Park.

Boom!

Before the Bomb the flowers grow the meadows full
   of life,
the bluebird sings,

217

the fruit tree brings in
pounds and pounds of food,
the creatures roam throughout the wood
and kids go swimming as they should,
the lamb it bleats,
the farm makes wheat,
and nature's all so real.
A lion's lair is very rare to be intruded much
but after bombing it's
au contraire, there is no mighty lion's lair.
The flowers and the bluebird dead
and for the trees not much is said
the creatures gone,
the kids forlorn
for the waters don't exist.
A lamb, what's that?
And what's a farm?
Nature is fantasy
all worldy goods are long forgot
and ancient cultures left to rot.
The ashes scattered on the ground
remains of boy and dog,
the charred remains of buildings stand
engulfed in heavy fog,
and the oceans are polluted so that people dare not fish.
I wish to stop
I wish to halt
this nutty foolishness.
— Ben Neaderland (E)

Occasional Poems can be written in anticipation of an event (perhaps to be read at a ceremony) or as a response to an occurrence (such as Tennyson's "Charge of the Light Brigade"). When I was writer-in-residence at the Interlochen Arts Academy, I encouraged my workshop students to write Occasional Poems for use in the school. Their topical collaborations included a birthday poem for the chairman of the department, a Thanksgiving Grace (which was recited at the Thanksgiving dinner for the students who were unable to go home), and a dedication poem for the Chapel/Recital Hall. At P.S. 75 in Manhattan my students wrote a dedication poem for the renovated playground (which was named after a teacher who had died).

The Soul of the Playground

Our playground was designed partly by the minds of children.
Built for the energy
that comes from children.

It's a lovely place to play with my friends
or sometimes I come here to sort out my thoughts.

When I play in the playground
my harness has been taken off,
giving me luxurious freedom.
In the playground I get the feeling
that I'm teasing the school.
It's a playful tease not a mean tease.

When you have bad feelings you can let them out
by running swift and fearless
and letting your bad feeings perish
into the flames of the past.
I feel like the playground changes colors
and I change with them.

The climbing structure is wood instead of metal,
which is good because wood doesn't get cold and clammy.
The slide may be your invisible unicorn that flies way above the stars.
Laughter echoes through the trees.
The new playground looks like a lucky kid's backyard.
You can pour out your soul
to the playground
because it will listen.

Part Two

Mrs. Freeman was a friend to everyone she taught.
Even the bad kids.
At 3:00 you had to leave her, I never wanted to.
When she died I first noticed how beat up the playground was.
Most of the first and second graders won't know who she is
because they weren't around,
but we're sure they'll understand how special she was and how much
        people loved her.
Yellow roses and Mrs. Freeman really go together.

Mrs. Freeman was
teaching from a heart that
still was partly child
for the children, to make their lives worthwhile.
So it is only right
to dedicate this playground
to Mrs. Freeman.
                    — Class collaboration
                    Carole Karasik's fifth/sixth grade class

    I like the collaboration approach when students are writing for a
local occasion. All students can be invited to contribute, and you or a student can combine the best parts. This enables several students to share in the
event, and the selection process results in a strong piece.

Poet Joel Oppenheimer has made Occasional Poems a major part of his oeuvre, including this one from his book *On Occasion:*

A Wedding

(for gordon and sue, 29 december 1969)

like a film it
unfolds, reels
along, and we find
ourselves confronted:
this man, this
woman, facing each
other, hearts full, they
are facing each other,
they are saying the
words, they are committing
themselves to that
particular devotion,
that particular love
they have discovered.
take heart! they are
showing us that love exists!
they are showing us there
is some sanity left!
in a world like a film,
they are creating their own
world, they are carving
a space to live in, to
talk to someone else!
may they be blessed for
this, and prosper by it.

Write a poem about any social or political event or issue — international, national, or local.

Write a poem for an upcoming or recent occasion, such as a school or civic event, wedding, funeral, or birth.

Greeting Cards

It used to be difficult to find appropriate greeting cards for occasions such as birthdays and anniversaries; most cards were either sodden with detached sentimentality, or they leered with sexual double entendres. A new generation of more tasteful cards has entered the market, but store-bought cards can never be as personal as one you make yourself. Suggest that students create their own cards, consisting of poetry and visual images made to order for the occasion: a birthday poem that tells why this person is special, or an anniversary card with specifics relating to the celebrating couple.

73
Things I Don't Understand

Uncertainty is a strong impetus to write; good poems, stories, and essays are more likely to derive from question marks than exclamation points.

Ask the students to write about one or more things they don't understand. Some students need to be assured that they are being assigned to ask questions rather than come up with answers. This assignment can be adopted for all courses; future scientists and scholars should be able to articulate what they don't know, too.

After students have written their pieces, have each one exchange with a neighbor, who then tries to answer the questions raised. The answerer can assume an all-knowing persona and reply authoritatively (even if the answers are wild guesses). You can double-cross the class by having students answer their own questions.

Students might unearth material worth exploring further. Questions of human nature—such as, "Why are some people shy?"—can be investigated in a short story, while factual and theoretical questions can lead to library research springing from personal rather than assigned curiosity.

Things I Don't Understand

In the beginning I thought I knew about love. At least I felt that way. But then I started thinking, "Am I really in love?" I really don't know now. What is love? Is it loving your mother, caring, sharing, teaching? A sex fiend? Or is love all of these? How do you feel you love someone or how do you know if someone loves you? Do they love you only when they want you for your body?

—Connie (M)

My theory about love is many people don't really love each other. They are just attracted to one another. When you meet a cute boy you don't fall in love with that person, you are just attracted to him. Love isn't something that happens overnight; it takes time. Parents who get divorced are really not in love. At one time they thought they were in love but they were attracted to their bodies. Don't worry, Mr. Right will come along.

—Elizabeth Kelso (M)

I don't understand the splitting of the atom, the way a key on the piano makes sounds, and what's normal and abnormal about things that happen during teen years: the way people feel excitement, depression—their laughter and pain, confusion in time.

—Orchid (M)

No one can explain everything. But when you feel depressed, you might cheer up when you realize you are not the only one in the world with these questions.

—Jenny (M)

•

I don't understand why they make nuclear weapons. If there were a nuclear war there wouldn't be any winners. All life on this planet would be extinct. So what's the use of making these things if we aren't going to do anything but destroy ourselves with them?

—Fred Herman (M)

Some people are just stupid.

—Christine Marten (M)

74
Immersion

Select with your students a compelling subject area—such as the nuclear age, adolescence, racism, immigration, emigration, aging, or life in another culture or era—and immerse the class in literary and other sources regarding the topic. Through discussions, student research, dramatic improvisations, and guest speakers (if possible), turn the classroom into a sort of think tank.

All this information goes through the students' creative filters and comes out in various forms: essay, poem, story, drama, dance, drawing, and song. Through analytical thinking and artistic expression, students can come to a greater understanding of an important issue.

Brainstorm with the students about possible ways of researching and writing about the topic. You can designate a month to be devoted to the theme, and schedule a regular time period for work on the project, which can culminate in a publication, performance, or videotape. For example, the following activities and writing assignments apply to the subject of "aging":

Visit a nursing home, senior citizens' center, or park and interview old people about what their lives are like now and what they were like when they were your age. Ask them if they can show you mementos from their youth—a good foundation for a conversation. Collect stories from them. Ask them how being old compares with how they thought it would be.

Discuss the word "old" and its various connotations, as in "old friends," "old wine," "olden days," "old timer," and "old dog."

Bring in recent and old photographs of grandparents or other old people. (Biographies often include photographs of the subject at various ages.) Write about the changes.

Write metaphors for being old.

Discuss and write about how your attitudes toward your grandparents compare with the way you feel about other old people. (Kids often have warm, understanding feelings about their grandparents, but perceive the old man and woman down the street as crabby nuisances).

As a way of empathizing with the physical problems old people often have, write about a time you were incapacitated (with the flu or your leg in a cast), and try to imagine what it would be like to feel that way all the time. (This can be explored in a dramatic improvisation, perhaps with someone else playing a spry, impatient old person.)

Discuss and act out stereotypes of aging—facial expressions, movements, styles of dress, etc.—then spend some time observing and listening to old people. How does reality stack up against the stereotypes?

Write in the persona of an old person. Or write from the point of view of yourself in 60 years.

Write a dialogue between an old person and a kid; include a conflict between them and how they go about resolving it (they don't have to solve everything, but they should understand each other a little better at the end). Act it out in class and lead a discussion of your classmates' reactions.

Write "both sides of the coin" about being old and your opinions of old people.

Discuss society's role in caring for old people. To what extent is it a family or government responsibility? Write government officials for their opinions and copies of relevant legislation. What laws would you propose?

Research how different cultures perceive and treat old people.

Write a song directed to a grandparent or other old person.

The following song is from a WCBS-TV show about children's attitudes toward aging, "We Don't Act Our Age." The show was written and performed by one of my classes at P.S. 75, Carole Karasik's fifth/sixth grade class, using the Immersion approach.

Song

My grandma lost
Her prince charming
A very long time ago

But I am here
To comfort her
And that, I think, she knows

> If you would listen, Grandma,
> I would be overjoyed
> Please, Grandma, come and talk to me
> I won't ask for any toys

> I wish you would not sit there
> Just staring into space

224

Thinking only of the past
With a blank look on your face

Tell me a bedtime story
I'll listen quietly
Your stories never bore me
I will take it carefully

Please, Grandma, tell a story
Nice so I do not weep
Long so I get drowsy
Sweet so I'll fall asleep

My grandma lost
Her prince charming
A very long time ago

But I am here
To comfort her
And that, I think, she knows

—Tyra Johnston and Elizabeth Freeman (E)

75
Myths, Fables, and Legends

Myths, fables, and legends (forms which are similar in structure) have been around as long as people have wondered "why?" and have been fascinated with exploits and adventures. Besides having anthropological and psychological significance, these tales are *good stories,* captivating audiences with exotic settings, larger-than-life action, and primal conflicts.

Jung's concept of the "collective unconscious" is supported by the fact that cultures with no mutual contact have come up wth similar myths and legends. Some common themes are: explanations of origins (including creation); the quest; traveling through time; the god or king disguised as a common person; and explanations of natural phenomena.

Myths, fables, and legends — like dreams — can exaggerate, connect the disconnected, and work symbolically. Any library contains a great deal of material on this subject, which you can draw on to create a unit on these magical stories.

The exponential increase in scientific information has lessened the need for explanatory myths, but students can put down the science book and come up with new myths for old phenomena. *Write a new myth to explain anything that might have baffled primitive people, including how things got to be the way they are (how did the sun get into the sky?) and why things happen (why does the sun disappear every night?).*

How the Sun Came to Be
Trillions of years ago the world was black because the evil spirits were covering the sun. A man named Zenders decided to take the evil spirits away from the sun. He leaped up and dove into the black spirits and landed on a star. Then Zenders reached for the sun. He squished the spirits. The spirits

turned into black dust, and the dust landed on earth. Ever since then the dust made a mighty fine soil for the sun to shine on!

—Jennifer Agro (E)

Why Wolves Howl at the Moon

It was a dark misty night. All the wolves were quiet. They were watching the wolf god catch their food. He was chasing a giant rabbit. The rabbit just got away, and jumped all the way to the moon. The wolf god followed. All the wolves in the world were watching. The god never came back. For hours all the wolves gave long, loud and screeching howls. And that's why they howl at the moon.

—Chris Delmond (E)

Write a myth to explain a recent pheonomenon, such as the origin of the microchip or video games.

Write in the form of a fable or legend. A fable is a supernatural story that makes a moral point, often using animals as characters. A legend is a story that comes down from the past, usually about extraordinary exploits, perhaps with some historical basis.

•

Every school and community has its legends—stories that get told and retold, made out of varying blends of truth and fiction. Write any local legends you know, or try to find some by talking to older students, teachers, or local residents. A senior citizens' center is an ideal place to go looking for good stories. Or, make up a legend or myth set in the community.

76
Reasons

Write five reasons to write and five reasons not to write.

Don't be afraid of contradictions: profound contradictions are paradoxes, and are expected from any writer of depth. You can give reasons you currently feel, once felt, or you think others feel. Reasons can be temporary ("I have a headache") or ongoing ("The world doesn't need any more mediocre poems").

This assignment tends not to produce writing that can stand up on its own, but it can serve as a springboard for a discussion on attitudes toward writing. When the negative reasons are read aloud, students are reminded that others share the same problems and doubts; perhaps they can offer each other ways of coping, or, at least, commiseration. (If not, just complaining can feel good.) The reasons *for* writing can inspire other students, perhaps by rekindling enthusiasm.

77
Don't Write

The original reason I did this assignment was selfish: I needed a few minutes of quiet. The day was hectic, the class was noisy, and I wanted everybody to shut up for a while; no questions, no complaints. I asked the class to stop everything—no writing, no talking, no movement out of their seats. Nothing for three minutes. I gave them no other instructions.

After it was over—it seemed longer than three minutes—I asked them to write about what had happened internally (inside their heads and bodies) and/or externally (around the room). Some of the students chronicled their experience during the silent period, and others worked on ideas generated during what was, in effect, an enforced prewriting segment. Here is an excerpt:

> ...I looked at the ceiling and the floor to see if I could discover anything ....My mind was absolutely blank. But as I come to think of it, after a few minutes were up I was full of ideas. My mind is a wavy line.
> —Isabel Feliz (E)

I repeated this kind of session with other classes; it evolved into the following sequence: 1) Five minutes of silence. 2) Five minutes of writing about what happened. 3) Fifteen (or more) minutes of follow-up writing, when students can add to or refine what they have written.

78
Poetic License

The term *poetic license* is often used facetiously ("They ought to revoke your poetic license for that lousy metaphor"; "I can't write today because I forgot to renew my poetic license") Ask students to take the term literally, though not necessarily seriously, by writing their versions of such a license, including the rights, privileges, and obligations of being a poet. You can read the Hippocratic Oath to the class as an example of a professional code, and, for a more succinct credo, this poem by Ron Padgett:

Poetic License

This license certifies
That Ron Padgett may tell whatever lies
His heart desires
Until it expires

•

Poetic License

I can say things I don't want
people to hear
and disguise them in my poetry.
That is what makes writing mysterious.

I have the ability
to make up life and death
in a pencil and paper.
I can turn the nice dreams
into nightmares.

Because I am a writer
I get to have
more than one notebook.

I have the right
to take your face, your body,
and your personality
and put them on paper;
make people heroes or enemies,
happy or sad, crazy or sane.

I can change the emotions
of thousands
simply with a stroke
of my pen.

I have the right to examine you
to find the truth
but, because I am a writer,
I don't have to tell the truth.

I have the right to create, re-create,
write and rewrite.
I have the right to walk down the street
taking notes on everything I see;
it doesn't matter whether I like it or not.

I am a writer,
someone with a third eye
to see things
left unseen by others.
Someone with a third hand
to hold things
left unfound by others.

Writing means a dozen thoughts
bunched up in only a few words.
Everything held inside of me
slips out as easily as fish can swim.

I imagine something totally impossible —
my pen dances on the paper
making it real.

With a pen
I can get away with

anything!

— Class collaboration
Carole Karasik's fifth/sixth grade class

79
Collaborations

A true collaboration can result in a whole greater than the sum of the participants. When the lonely task of writing becomes a collaborative venture, sparks often fly—sparks of creative electricity and/or sparks of artistic disagreement. Collaborating takes the loneliness out of writing, and has other benefits. It can be a good diversion when a student needs a break from his or her own writing or is suffering from writer's block. Also, writers of contrasting styles can team up and absorb new possibilities from each other. Finally, the collaborative process can be a laboratory for cooperation and communication; see what happens when two "enemies" collaborate.

What follows are some collaborative assignments. Keep in mind that *any* assignment can be handled collaboratively, and any of these collaborative assignments can be tackled individually. These particular assignments, however, lend themselves well to collaboration because they tend to profit from diverse inputs. Students can work in pairs or small groups, or you can orchestrate collaborations with the full class.

Leaping Collaborations

A linguistic or conceptual leap can startle the writer as well as the reader. This poem by Gregory Orr hops from line one to line two, then leaps to line three:

Washing My Face

Last night's dreams disappear.
They are like the sink draining:
a transparent rose swallowed by its stem.

232

For Leaping Collaborations, one student writes two lines, then a partner adds a third line, which can be a hop, skip, jump, or flying leap from the first two. Perhaps this is best demonstrated by examples:

Birds are chirping in the summer sun
Dogs are barking in the winter snow

The Pet Store, where little animals are trying to get out
— Lisa Bracero, Paul McGirt (E)

A scoop of pistachio ice cream
some whipped cream

A polar bear on a bush
— Anonymous (E)

Sprinkles fall upon ice cream cones
lickety lick they're gone, the licks become sharper

and harder, a snake
— Anonymous (E)

Chimneys throwing smoke for heat
People freezing and buying

The grocery owner was a farmer and he wants to be young again
— Edwin Zapata, Antonio Gonzales (E)

Invent a Poet

Sleeping Obsessions, a book of poems by Mercy Bona, came out in 1978. Many of the poems had appeared in literary magazines, and one reviewer wrote that "Bona writes poems which. . . leave stodgy academics sitting in the dust counting their adjectives." Mercy Bona was asked to give a reading. But Bona couldn't be there — or anywhere else — because there was no Mercy Bona. Or rather, Mercy Bona was three of us, which was hinted at by the epigraph to *Sleeping Obsessions:* "I led three lives."

The poems were written collaboratively by Harry Greenberg, Larry Zirlin, and myself, using various approaches. The most common technique was for two or all three of us to take turns on a poem until someone declared it to be finished. A second method was for one of us to sit at the typewriter while the other two threw around lines; the typist would decide which lines to include, revising them and adding his own lines as he pleased. A third approach was for one of us to hand over a fragment or an abandoned poem and say, "See if you can do anything with this." A Mercy Bona "voice" emerged and got stronger. An unspoken rule prohibited arguing unless the disagreement was major; final decisions were made by whoever typed the final copy.

Mercy Bona is not the only fictitious poet around. A creative writing class taught by poet Robert Hershon invented poet Lawrence Stazer (an anagram of "ersatz"), who gave a triumphant reading for unsuspecting schoolmates. Appropriately, Larry Zirlin (one-third of Mercy) was called on to play the guest poet.

Your students can invent their own collaborative poets in small groups, or the whole class can contribute to a single make-believe author. These phantom poets should have their own folders, into which students insert fragments which are up for grabs. They might want to agree on some biographical and literary facts about the writer(s), as in this fictitious contributor's note: "Born and raised on a farm, he moved to New York City, where he worked as a cab driver and consultant to the United Nations. His writing is highly influenced by television commercials and Greek myths."

A twist on this project is to invent a poet who writes in another language, and to collaborate on "translations" of this newly discovered writer: "Although she had a devoted following in 18th-century France, her manuscripts were only recently discovered. . . ."

Invent a Poet is a good project for students having trouble with their own writing. When your voice doesn't work, try someone else's. (It turns out to be you, too.) A project like this can inject energy into a listless group, perhaps with the fun of a hoax publication and/or poetry reading to look forward to.

Invent a Monster Story

Younger students love being amazed, entertained, and scared by monsters, so it's no surprise that famous monsters show up in their writings. I started to tire of King Kong, Godzilla, Frankenstein's monster, and other hairy, scaly, or bulging behemoths being lifted whole from celluloid to paper: "Look," I told a fourth grade seminar group, "if you're going to write about monsters, they should be your own."

I defined *monster* loosely as any creature not natural to the planet, and asked for suggestions for a collaborative monster. We had fun, and, like eating potato chips, it was hard to stop at one (Dr. Frankenstein must have had great self-control). Before we did another, I pointed out that we had created an evil monster, but there is another dimension to monsters. Watching the classy monster movies, audiences feel some empathy for the creature, who is often a misunderstood victim of circumstances or exploitation (King Kong didn't book a tour to the top of the Empire State Building). The group then created a nice, naive sister for the first monster, and they named the siblings Buster and Poohster Goggles.

The energy was so high that we embarked on a collaborative project utilizing Buster and Poohster. We arrived at an overview of their character traits, and then I asked for titles for vignettes about their lives. I wrote the titles on the board and each student picked one. At the beginning of each subsequent session I read the vignettes from the previous session before asking for more titles.

A storyline developed, with the vignettes being divided among general categories such as School, Romance, Jobs, and Heroics. In the final sections, Buster and Poohster split up, only to be reunited in the end, with Buster nicer and Poohster wiser. The students beamed like proud parents because their "kids" had turned out all right after all. We published a sampling of the vignettes in a booklet called "The Monster Chronicles."

This was the first sustained writing experience for this group, and my first as a teacher. For the first time, a writing project wasn't finished because the bell rang, and the students knew what they'd be working on before they entered the room the next time.

This approach need not, of course, be limited to monsters.

Invent a Magazine

Think of a subject that has not had its own magazine. If you suggested "gourmet bathing," then you don't know about *Wet*. I've seen a magazine devoted to the glories of baldness, and I've heard about a periodical for parking-lot owners, with advertisements for tickets, painted lines, and asphalt.

With all the magazines on the market, it would seem that every interest has been covered sufficiently, but new magazines keep showing up. Ask the class to find a likely (or unlikely) theme for a new magazine, and then do a sample issue, including cover, table of contents, a few articles, advertisements, editorials, etc. Or, students can satirize an existing magazine or genre of magazines (the *Us-People* syndrome, beauty magazines, sports, etc.).

Here are some possible titles: *Canine— The Magazine by and for Dogs; Children's Liberation; Adolescent Secrets; Snackworld.*

Another possibility is to follow the trend of magazines about individual cities *(New York, Los Angeles, Houston, Philadelphia),* and create a magazine for your location. If you live in a city, you might want to focus on the school's part of town. The magazine could include restaurant reviews, a guide to local hangouts, interviews with local officials and shopkeepers, and "mood" pieces on the area's atmosphere (using the Place and Eavesdropping assignments in chapters 51 and 29).

Set aside a folder for all material related to the magazine. If it shapes up, perhaps you can publish it for local distribution. The *Foxfire* books show how much can be done when students write about their communities.

Smorgasbord Sonnet

I learned this sneaky exercise from poet Harry Greenberg. Take fourteen index cards of slips or paper and number them. Your part of the collaboration is to write — on the lower right hand corner of each card — the end-word of each line of an Elizabethan sonnet (which is divided into three four-line stanzas, follwed by a couplet; the rhyme scheme is ABAB, CDCD, EFEF, GG). Therefore, the word on index card 1 rhymes with 3; 2 rhymes with 4; and so on, with 13 rhyming with 14.

Hand out the cards to fourteen students; or, make two sets and give them to twenty-eight students. Tell them each to write one line, ending with the word on his or her card, but don't tell them why. I dispense with iambic pentameter and allow the students to write as many syllables as they like, provided the line doesn't get too long. You can give the students a theme ("School," "Play," "Beyond Dreams," "My Hometown"), to which you have tailored your end-words, or you can make it open-ended. Students can start lines with conjnctions.

Collect the cards and put them in order. You now have a rhymed, Elizabethan sonnet—minus meter. Any connections between lines will be random, and, if you didn't give the students a theme, any overall cohesiveness will be by chance. Explain the sonnet form and ʳead the poem out loud as forcefully and seriously as possible, as if the poem had deep meaning and every line flowed naturally into the next. (Practice or read it silently first; you may wish to make minor syntactical revisions to help the poem flow.) The Smorgasbord Sonnet has never failed to produce at least a couple of startling connections between lines.

This is a good activity for times when some of the students are working and others are idle; if only a few students are available, you can double up on the cards. The following sample was written by a workshop of teachers; the theme I gave them was "education":

On Education

She opened her mouth and let out a splash.
Kierkegaard is boring!!!
Books and bodies crash.
Reading scores take off like seagulls soaring.

No thoughts, no words, what a dummy!
Ideas shooting thru her mind—an explosion.
Touch it, it's crummy.
Ideas dropping into children's minds...erosion.

Preach, don't teach.
The earth doesn't think, it can just create.
Teach, don't preach.
Happiness, why do you be late?

Their brains are smart, tho sometimes they talk like fools.
All this and more goes on in schools.

Collaborative Story

Through group process you can explore the elements of story-making, as was done in the Invent a Monster collaboration. Sometimes I go into a class and ask for an opening element—a character, conflict, or setting—which, through nurturing, can grow into a story.

In one fifth grade class, my call for a starter was met by "an exorcist." The movie of the same name had been on television the night before, and I suggested that it would be difficult to write about an exorcist without being overly influenced by the movie. I asked them what the word "exorcist" made them think of, and someone called out "the devil." I asked for a second character, and "the devil's son" was suggested.

After writing the two characters' names on the board, I asked for a general tone — mystery, comedy, drama, romance — and the consensus was for comedy. "How old is the devil's son?" Three voices responded: five, ten, and twenty-six. We took a vote, and twenty-six won. I asked for a picture of this twenty-six-year-old devil's son: "He has a moustache and wears a tuxedo." Now we needed a premise upon which to build a story. "What if he gets a job as a fireman?" said one student. "Yeah," added another, "that would really get his father angry."

A discussion followed about this father/son conflict, and we created a dialogue between the devil and his son when the son announces his choice of occupation, followed by a discussion of a typical day in this atypical household. At this point, we started to get diminishing returns from the group process, and I told the students that individually they could do whatever they wanted with the collaboratively developed material. This resulted in many stories with shared elements, rather than one unified collaboration.

80
One Especially for Teachers

Here's an assignment for teachers, which you can work on during those rare moments when all the students are actively engaged with their writing, and no one needs your advice and support.

When you first set eyes on a class in September, students are barely distinguishable from one another. Gradually, the faces become familiar and get connected with names. Over the course of the year, images and feelings accumulate for each individual, until June brings dissolution of the family. Each September brings new students, and those from past years may become blurred. This assignment can help you keep them in focus.

Write a series of short sketches for each student, using physical description, behavioral and verbal patterns, and comparisons. Look around the room until a line or an image comes to you regarding a particular student. Do one or two sketches at a time until you have a class portrait in words to complement the class photograph. These sketches are by Sia Lazos about her sixth grade students at P.S. 173 in Manhattan:

> Dark, innocent eyes
> Looking up through two clear panes
> Eyeglasses taped to stay together
> Where lunchtime stresses
> Have broken them
>
> "Oh," she said
> "I thought you meant something else"
> "OH" "Oh" "oh"

Jack-in-the-Box
Indefatigable
Smiling, sneering, all sounds imitating
Running 'round the room
With someone else's anything

Perfectionist, striving, reaching
reworking, remodelling
Talent bursting forth in all directions
But not ever satisfied

81
Be a Writer

The goal of the writing workshop is to engender self-confidence through familiarity with the writing process and subject matter, so it is fitting that the last assignment in this book is the one most writers start with.

Be a writer. Conceive of something to write about, and write it. Or, write in order to conceive of something to write about.

The overall response to this assignment may be a barometer of a workshop's ongoing success, but any individual failures only indicate that those students are sharing the experience, at that very moment, of countless other writers around the world.

Loneliness sounds like . . . . (image).

Some good assignments :

BIBLIOGRAPHY

Many of the literary references in this book are credited in the permissions section. The following books provided helpful background material for *The Writing Workshop: Volume 2.* (See also the more extensive bibliography in *The Writing Workshop: Volume 1.)*

Agee, James. *The Collected Short Prose of James Agee,* edited by Robert Fitzgerald. Boston: Houghton Mifflin, 1968.

Arieti, Silvano. *Creativity.* New York: Basic Books, 1976.

Beckson, Karl and Ganz, Arthur. *Literary Terms: A Dictionary.* New York: Farrar, Straus and Giroux, 1975.

Jacob, Max. *Advice to a Young Poet.* London: Menard Press, 1976.

Jung, C.G. *The Spirit in Man, Art, and Literature.* Translated by R.F.C. Hull. Princeton, N.J.: Princeton University Press, 1971.

Lopate, Phillip. *Being with Children.* New York: Doubleday, 1975.

Mayakovsky, Vladimir. *How Are Verses Made?* London: Jonathan Cape, 1970.

Mencken, H.L. *The American Language.* New York: Alfred A. Knopf, 1979.

Preminger, Alex, ed. *Princeton Encyclopedia of Poetry and Poetics.* Princeton, N.J.: Princeton University Press, 1974.

Schlauch, Margaret. *The Gift of Language.* New York: Dover, 1955.

Sternburg, Janet and Ziegler, Alan. "A Conversation with Charles Reznikoff." In *Montemora No. 2,* edited by Geoffrey O'Brien and Eliot Weinberger. New York: The Montemora Foundation, 1976.

Thompson, Denys. *The Uses of Poetry.* Cambridge: Cambridge University Press, 1978.

Wheelock, John Hall, ed. *Editor to Author: The Letters of Maxwell E. Perkins.* New York: Scribners, 1965.

ABOUT THE AUTHOR

Alan Ziegler has been conducting writing workshops for Teachers & Writers Collaborative since 1974 and also teaches at Columbia University. He has taught for Poets in the Schools, Poets & Writers, and Bronx Community College, and has conducted writing residencies at the Interlochen Arts Academy and Hampshire College. He has a masters degree in creative writing from The City College of New York, where he studied with Kurt Vonnegut and Joel Oppenheimer.

Mr. Ziegler has lectured on the teaching of writing for the NCTE, Vassar College, Adelphi University, Loyola University, the New York City Board of Education, and others. He is coordinator of Writers-in-Lynbrook, a district-wide program of writing workshops in the Lynbrook (Long Island) school district, and has worked extensively with teachers. Poetry by his students comprises the text of *Almost Grown,* a book of photographs of teenagers by Joseph Szabo. He was creative consultant to "We Don't Act Our Age" (WCBS-TV), which won a N.Y. Emmy Award for Outstanding Children's Programming.

Mr. Ziegler's books include *So Much To Do,* a collection of poetry, and *The Writing Workshop: Volume I.* His poetry and prose have appeared in such publications as *Paris Review, The Village Voice, The New York Times, The Ardis Anthology of New American Poetry, American Poetry Review,* and *The New American Review,* and he has written for the Ragabash Puppet Theater. Two of his stories were selected for the PEN/NEA Syndicated Fiction Project. He received a N.Y. State CAPS grant in poetry, and co-edited *Some* literary magazine and Release Press. Mr. Ziegler is currently writing a novel.